# GOD'S
# WORDS
*of* COMFORT

# GOD'S
# WORDS
## *of* COMFORT

### BIBLE PASSAGES TO CALM YOUR FEARS
### AND FEED YOUR SOUL

BETHANY HOUSE PUBLISHERS
*a division of Baker Publishing Group*
Minneapolis, Minnesota

© 2012 by Bethany House Publishers

Compiled by Barbara Kois
Series editor: Andy McGuire

Published by Bethany House Publishers
11400 Hampshire Avenue South
Bloomington, Minnesota 55438
www.bethanyhouse.com

Bethany House Publishers is a division of
Baker Publishing Group, Grand Rapids, Michigan

Printed in the United States of America

Library of Congress Cataloging-in-Publication Data

God's words of comfort : Bible passages to calm your fears and feed your soul.
   p.  cm.
   Includes bibliographical references.
   Summary: "A collection of Bible quotations that offer encouragement and hope in times of grief, loneliness, illness, failure, fear, and similar situations"—Provided by publisher.
   ISBN 978-0-7642-1025-9 (pbk. : alk. paper)
   1. Suffering—Biblical teaching. 2. Consolation—Biblical teaching. 3. Encouragement—Biblical teaching. 4. Bible—Quotations. I. Bethany House Publishers.
BS680.S854G63 2012
242'.4—dc23
          2012013962

12   13   14   15   16   17   18       7  6  5  4  3  2  1

# Contents

# Introduction

Hurricanes, wildfires, tornados, earthquakes. Job loss, financial reversal, health problems, broken relationships. The storms of life—are you in one right now?

Today we hear of violent weather, deteriorating economic conditions, and disastrous relationships. Many of these are utterly beyond our control.

How great it is to know the One who calms the storm, the One so powerful that the wind and waves obey Him: Jesus. He also calms our hearts and eases our fears.

But sometimes the storms rage so loudly and the damage done by them is so profound that it's hard to hear His voice or experience the comfort He offers each one of us during every storm . . . and in times of peace as well.

God's Word, the Bible, is full of comfort for the difficult times of life. This book gathers them up for you and makes them easy to find, even when you're blown and buffeted by the storm.

May God's comforting words be a balm for your soul.

# 1

## God's Word in Times of Grief

When you come to the place where you recognize that
everything you have and everyone you love is a gift, it be-
comes possible to enjoy those gifts—not with an attitude
of greed but with one of gratitude. You and I, like Job, know
that God gives and God takes away. And when he takes
away, if we're able to focus on the joy of what was given,
if only for a time, we take another step down the pathway
toward the heart of God.[1]

*—Holding on to Hope*

Few of us are called on to suffer the shattering losses of Job.
On one day, he lost all of his children, his possessions, and
his health. Yet many of us have had the experience of a day
that changed our world drastically and/or permanently. Or
we may have experienced, like Job, emotional or physical
abandonment by a spouse or friends.

Yet instead of asking "Why me?" as is tempting at a time of tragedy, Job in his shock and grief, said, "Blessed be the name of the Lord." The Bible says that through all of his suffering and grief, he did not sin nor blame God.

Instead, even in the depths of his grief, he was able to say, "Though He slay me, yet will I trust in Him." Now *that* is faith—faith that is available to all who will put their trust in Him.

~~~~~

When they cry out to me, I will hear, for I am compassionate.
(**EXODUS 22:27** NIV)

———

The LORD is my shepherd; I shall not want. He maketh me to lie down in green pastures: he leadeth me beside the still waters.

He restoreth my soul: he leadeth me in the paths of righteousness for his name's sake.

Yea, though I walk through the valley of the shadow of death, I will fear no evil: for thou art with me; thy rod and thy staff they comfort me.

Thou preparest a table before me in the presence of mine enemies: thou anointest my head with oil; my cup runneth over.

Surely goodness and mercy shall follow me all the days of my life: and I will dwell in the house of the LORD for ever.
(**PSALM 23** KJV)

*This psalm expresses David's personal confidence, joy, and triumph like no other. As a shepherd, he naturally relates God's care for us to David's care for his sheep. He looks forward with the same hope we can have today—hope in God and His promises.*

———

Forsake me not, O Lord; O my God, be not far from me. Make haste to help me, O Lord, my Salvation. (**PSALM 38:21–22 AMP**)

———

I will turn their mourning into joy and will comfort them and give them joy for their sorrow. (**JEREMIAH 31:13 NASB**)

*Joy is not dependent on circumstances like happiness is. Joy comes from faith in God and His sovereignty. Here He makes one of His ironclad promises—to provide comfort and joy.*

## —THE BEATITUDES—

And seeing the multitudes, He went up on a mountain, and when He was seated His disciples came to Him. Then He opened His mouth and taught them, saying:

"Blessed are the poor in spirit, for theirs is the kingdom of heaven.

Blessed are those who mourn, for they shall be comforted.

Blessed are the meek, for they shall inherit the earth.

Blessed are those who hunger and thirst for righteousness, for they shall be filled.

Blessed are the merciful, for they shall obtain mercy.

Blessed are the pure in heart, for they shall see God.

Blessed are the peacemakers, for they shall be called sons of God.

Blessed are those who are persecuted for righteousness' sake, for theirs is the kingdom of heaven.

Blessed are you when they revile and persecute you, and say all kinds of evil against you falsely for My sake.

Rejoice and be exceedingly glad, for great is your reward in heaven, for so they persecuted the prophets who were before you" (**MATTHEW 5:1–12 NKJV**).

*The word used here for blessed indicates an inward state and can mean "happy." But some of the states Jesus describes here as "blessed" don't sound very happy to us—those who mourn, those who are persecuted for righteousness' sake. But all of the qualities listed in this passage flow from the first—those who recognize that they are poor or even bankrupt spiritually turn to God and rely on His mercy and grace. Then He provides the peace, comfort, and purity of heart that result from our dependence upon Him.*

———

Come to Me, all who are weary and heavy-laden, and I will give you rest.

Take My yoke upon you, and learn from Me, for I am gentle and humble in heart; and you will find rest for your souls.

For My yoke is easy, and My burden is light. (**MATTHEW 11:28–30 NASB**)

———

Jesus answered and said to her, "Everyone who drinks of this water will thirst again; but whoever drinks of the water that I will give him shall never thirst; but the water that I will give him will become in him a well of water springing up to eternal life" (JOHN 4:13–14 NASB).

———

I assure you: Anyone who hears My word and believes Him who sent Me has eternal life and will not come under judgment but has passed from death to life.

I assure you: An hour is coming, and is now here, when the dead will hear the voice of the Son of God, and those who hear will live.

For just as the Father has life in Himself, so also He has granted to the Son to have life in Himself.

And He has granted Him the right to pass judgment, because He is the Son of Man.

Do not be amazed at this, because a time is coming when all who are in the graves will hear His voice and come out—those who have done good things, to the resurrection of life, but those who have done wicked things, to the resurrection of judgment.

I can do nothing on My own. I judge only as I hear, and My judgment is righteous, because I do not seek My own will, but the will of Him who sent Me. (JOHN 5:24–30 HCSB)

*Here Jesus sees God's wonderful future plan for all those who were spiritually dead but have been made alive through their faith. All people will be resurrected, either to life or to judgment, depending on what their response has been to Jesus Christ. If they believed, they will have life; if they have rejected Him, they will face judgment.*

———

My sheep hear My voice, and I know them, and they follow Me.

And I give them eternal life, and they shall never perish; neither shall anyone snatch them out of My hand.

My Father, who has given them to Me, is greater than all; and no one is able to snatch them out of My Father's hand. (**JOHN 10:27–29** NKJV)

———

"Let not your hearts be troubled. Believe in God; believe also in me.

In my Father's house are many rooms. If it were not so, would I have told you that I go to prepare a place for you?

And if I go and prepare a place for you, I will come again and will take you to myself, that where I am you may be also.

And you know the way to where I am going."

Thomas said to him, "Lord, we do not know where you are going. How can we know the way?"

Jesus said to him, "I am the way, and the truth, and the life. No one comes to the Father except through me" (**JOHN 14:1–6** ESV).

*As Jesus says good-bye to His disciples, He urges them to trust in the Father despite the difficulties they will face.*

I am the true vine, and My Father is the vineyard keeper. Every branch in Me that does not produce fruit He removes, and He prunes every branch that produces fruit so that it will produce more fruit.

You are already clean because of the word I have spoken to you. Remain in Me, and I in you. Just as a branch is unable to produce fruit by itself unless it remains on the vine, so neither can you unless you remain in Me.

I am the vine; you are the branches. The one who remains in Me and I in him produces much fruit, because you can do nothing without Me.

If anyone does not remain in Me, he is thrown aside like a branch and he withers. They gather them, throw them into the fire, and they are burned.

If you remain in Me and My words remain in you, ask whatever you want and it will be done for you.

My Father is glorified by this: that you produce much fruit and prove to be My disciples.

As the Father has loved me, I have also loved you. Remain in My love. If you keep My commands you will remain in My love, just as I have kept My Father's commands and remain in His love.

I have spoken these things to you so that My joy may be in you and your joy may be complete. This is My command: Love one another as I have loved you.

No one has greater love than this, that someone would lay down his life for his friends. You are My friends if you do what I command you.

I do not call you slaves anymore, because a slave doesn't know what his master is doing. I have called you friends, because I have made known to you everything I have heard from My Father.

You did not choose Me, but I chose you. I appointed you that you should go out and produce fruit and that your fruit should remain, so that whatever you ask the Father in My name, He will give you.

This is what I command you: Love one another. (**JOHN 15:1–17** HCSB)

*The vine and branches metaphor can be comforting in times of stress, hardship, or tragedy. Although the pruning of fruitful branches or cutting away of unfruitful branches is painful, it produces stronger, more fruitful vines in the long run. The key for the remaining branches is to remain firmly attached to the life-giving vine so that they have the nourishment needed to produce fruit.*

———

And so, dear brothers and sisters, we can boldly enter heaven's Most Holy Place because of the blood of Jesus. By his death, Jesus opened a new and life-giving way through the curtain into the Most Holy Place. And since we have a great High Priest who rules over God's house, let us go right into the presence of God with sincere hearts fully trusting him. For our guilty consciences have been sprinkled with Christ's blood to make us clean, and our bodies have been washed with pure water.

Let us hold tightly without wavering to the hope we affirm, for God can be trusted to keep his promise. Let us think of ways to motivate one another to acts of love and good works. And let us not neglect our meeting together, as some people do, but encourage one another, especially now that the day of his return is drawing near. (**HEBREWS 10:19–25 NLT**)

> *Holding fast to our hope is what we need to do in hard times. Paul tells us not to give up! Don't waiver. And don't withdraw—spend time with other believers so that you can encourage one another.*

———

Now faith is the assurance of things hoped for, the conviction of things not seen. (**HEBREWS 11:1 NASB**)

———

After these things I looked, and behold, a door standing open in heaven, and the first voice which I had heard, like the sound of a trumpet speaking with me, said, "Come up here, and I will show you what must take place after these things." Immediately I was in the Spirit; and behold, a throne was standing in heaven, and One sitting on the throne. And He who was sitting was like a jasper stone and a sardius in appearance; and there was a rainbow around the throne, like an emerald in appearance. Around the throne were twenty-four thrones; and upon the thrones I saw twenty-four elders sitting, clothed in white garments, and golden crowns on their heads.

Out from the throne come flashes of lightning and sounds and peals of thunder. And there were seven lamps of fire burning before the throne, which are the seven Spirits of God; and before the throne there was something like a sea of glass, like crystal; and in the center and around the throne, four living creatures full of eyes in front and behind. The first creature was like a lion, and the second creature like a calf, and the third creature had a face like that of a man, and the fourth creature was like a flying eagle. And the four living creatures, each one of them having six wings, are full of eyes around and within; and day and night they do not cease to say,

"HOLY, HOLY, HOLY IS THE LORD GOD, THE AL-MIGHTY, WHO WAS AND WHO IS AND WHO IS TO COME."

And when the living creatures give glory and honor and thanks to Him who sits on the throne, to Him who lives forever and ever, the twenty-four elders will fall down before Him who sits on the throne, and will worship Him who lives forever and ever, and will cast their crowns before the throne, saying,

"Worthy are You, our Lord and our God, to receive glory and honor and power; for You created all things, and because of Your will they existed, and were created" (**REVELATION 4 NASB**).

*After John has completed the letters to the seven churches of Asia, he is called up to the throne room in heaven where he sees God the Father on His throne. This passage has parallels with Ezekiel's vision, where he said, "The heavens were opened, and I*

*saw visions of God" (Ezekiel 1 KJV). This chapter prepares John*
*for the visions of the future to come in later chapters.*

———

Then I saw in the right hand of the One seated on the throne a scroll with writing on the inside and on the back, sealed with seven seals. I also saw a mighty angel proclaiming in a loud voice, "Who is worthy to open the scroll and break its seals?" But no one in heaven or on earth or under the earth was able to open the scroll or even to look in it. And I cried and cried because no one was found worthy to open the scroll or even to look in it.

Then one of the elders said to me, "Stop crying. Look! The Lion from the tribe of Judah, the Root of David, has been victorious so that He may open the scroll and its seven seals."

Then I saw one like a slaughtered lamb standing between the throne and the four living creatures and among the elders. He had seven horns and seven eyes, which are the seven spirits of God sent into all the earth. He came and took the scroll out of the right hand of the One seated on the throne.

When He took the scroll, the four living creatures and the 24 elders fell down before the Lamb. Each one had a harp and gold bowls filled with incense, which are the prayers of the saints. And they sang a new song:

You are worthy to take the scroll and to open its seals; because You were slaughtered, and You redeemed people for God by Your blood from every tribe and language and people and nation.

You made them a kingdom and priests to our God, and they will reign on the earth.

Then I looked, and heard the voice of many angels around the throne, and also of the living creatures and of the elders. Their number was countless thousands, plus thousands of thousands. They said with a loud voice:

The Lamb who was slaughtered is worthy to receive power and riches and wisdom and strength and honor and glory and blessing!

I heard every creature in heaven, on earth, under the earth, on the sea, and everything in them say:

Blessing and honor and glory and dominion to the One seated on the throne, and to the Lamb, forever and ever!

The four living creatures said, "Amen," and the elders fell down and worshiped. (REVELATION 5 HCSB)

*The scroll symbolizes God's covenant with mankind and the curses to come as a result of man's breaking that covenant. The curses will begin in chapter 6. John weeps because he desires to know the future of his beloved church and yet no one was able to open the book or scroll. Only the Lamb is able to take it from God's hand and He does. Note that the bowls filled with incense are the prayers of the saints (believers) and the heavenly assistants present them in heaven on our behalf.*

After this I saw four angels standing at the four corners of the earth, holding back the four winds of the earth to prevent any wind from blowing on the land or on the sea or on any tree. Then I saw another angel coming up from the east, having the seal of the living God. He called out in a loud voice to the four angels who had been given power to harm the land and the sea: "Do not harm the land or the sea or the trees until we put a seal on the foreheads of the servants of our God." Then I heard the number of those who were sealed: 144,000 from all the tribes of Israel.

From the tribe of Judah 12,000 were sealed,

from the tribe of Reuben 12,000,

from the tribe of Gad 12,000,

from the tribe of Asher 12,000,

from the tribe of Naphtali 12,000,

from the tribe of Manasseh 12,000,

from the tribe of Simeon 12,000,

from the tribe of Levi 12,000,

from the tribe of Issachar 12,000,

from the tribe of Zebulun 12,000,

from the tribe of Joseph 12,000,

from the tribe of Benjamin 12,000.

After this I looked, and there before me was a great multitude that no one could count, from every nation, tribe, people and language, standing before the throne and before the Lamb. They were wearing white robes and were holding palm branches in their hands. And they cried out in a loud voice:

"Salvation belongs to our God, who sits on the throne, and to the Lamb."

All the angels were standing around the throne and around the elders and the four living creatures. They fell down on their faces before the throne and worshiped God, saying:

"Amen! Praise and glory and wisdom and thanks and honor and power and strength be to our God for ever and ever. Amen!"

Then one of the elders asked me, "These in white robes—who are they, and where did they come from?"

I answered, "Sir, you know."

And he said, "These are they who have come out of the great tribulation; they have washed their robes and made them white in the blood of the Lamb. Therefore, they are before the throne of God and serve him day and night in his temple; and he who sits on the throne will shelter them with his presence. Never again will they hunger; never again will they thirst. The sun will not beat down on them, nor any scorching heat.

For the Lamb at the center of the throne will be their shepherd; he will lead them to springs of living water.

And God will wipe away every tear from their eyes" (**REVE-LATION 7 NIV**).

*John's vision is of four angels at the four points of the compass, holding four winds to prevent them from rushing in destruction upon the earth. These destructive powers are held back for a time from the earth until the preaching of the gospel can go forth and accomplish its desired result. The seal of the living God is a mark of His ownership and is thought to mean the public profession of faith in Christ. The last sentence indicates that when we are with God, all sorrow will be finished.*

## —THE NEW JERUSALEM—

Then I saw a new heaven and a new earth. The first heaven and the first earth had disappeared, and there was no sea anymore. And I saw the holy city, the new Jerusalem, coming down out of heaven from God. It was prepared like a bride dressed for her husband. And I heard a loud voice from the throne, saying, "Now God's presence is with people, and he will live with them, and they will be his people. God himself will be with them and will be their God. He will wipe away every tear from their eyes, and there will be no more death, sadness, crying, or pain, because all the old ways are gone."

The One who was sitting on the throne said, "Look! I am making everything new!" Then he said, "Write this, because these words are true and can be trusted."

The One on the throne said to me, "It is finished. I am the Alpha and the Omega, the Beginning and the End. I will give free water from the spring of the water of life to anyone who is thirsty. Those who win the victory will receive this, and I will be their God, and they will be my children. But cowards, those who refuse to believe, who do evil things, who kill, who sin sexually, who do evil magic, who worship idols, and who tell lies—all these will have a place in the lake of burning sulfur. This is the second death."

Then one of the seven angels who had the seven bowls full of the seven last troubles came to me, saying, "Come with me, and I will show you the bride, the wife of the Lamb." And the angel carried me away by the Spirit to a very large and high mountain. He showed me the holy city, Jerusalem, coming down out of heaven from God. It was shining with the glory of God and was bright like a very expensive jewel, like a jasper, clear as crystal. The city had a great high wall with twelve gates with twelve angels at the gates, and on each gate was written the name of one of the twelve tribes of Israel. There were three gates on the east, three on the north, three on the south, and three on the west. The walls of the city were built on twelve foundation stones, and on the stones were written the names of the twelve apostles of the Lamb.

The angel who talked with me had a measuring rod made of gold to measure the city, its gates, and its wall. The city was built in a square, and its length was equal to its width. The angel measured the city with the rod. The city was 1,500 miles long, 1,500 miles wide, and 1,500 miles high.

The angel also measured the wall. It was 216 feet high, by human measurements, which the angel was using. The wall was made of jasper, and the city was made of pure gold, as pure as glass. The foundation stones of the city walls were decorated with every kind of jewel. The first foundation was jasper, the second was sapphire, the third was chalcedony, the fourth was emerald, the fifth was onyx, the sixth was carnelian, the seventh was chrysolite, the eighth was beryl, the ninth was topaz, the tenth was chrysoprase, the eleventh was jacinth, and the twelfth was amethyst. The twelve gates were twelve pearls, each gate having been made from a single pearl. And the street of the city was made of pure gold as clear as glass.

I did not see a temple in the city, because the Lord God Almighty and the Lamb are the city's temple. The city does not need the sun or the moon to shine on it, because the glory of God is its light, and the Lamb is the city's lamp. By its light the people of the world will walk, and the kings of the earth will bring their glory into it. The city's gates will never be shut on any day, because there is no night there. The glory and the honor of the nations will be brought into it. Nothing unclean and no one who does shameful things or tells lies will ever go into it. Only those whose names are written in the Lamb's book of life will enter the city. (REVE-LATION 21 NCV)

> *The dead have been raised from the old earth, which was de-stroyed and replaced by a beautiful new place where God will wipe away every tear and there will be no more death, sadness, crying, or pain. Hallelujah!*

———

Then he showed me a river of the water of life, clear as crys-tal, coming from the throne of God and of the Lamb, in the middle of its street. On either side of the river was the tree of life, bearing twelve kinds of fruit, yielding its fruit every month; and the leaves of the tree were for the healing of the nations.

There will no longer be any curse; and the throne of God and of the Lamb will be in it, and His bond-servants will serve Him; they will see His face, and His name *will be* on their foreheads. And there will no longer be *any* night; and they will not have need of the light of a lamp nor the light of the sun, because the Lord God will illumine them; and they will reign forever and ever.

And he said to me, "These words are faithful and true; and the Lord, the God of the spirits of the prophets, sent His angel to show to His bond-servants the things which must soon take place.

And behold, I am coming quickly. Blessed is he who heeds the words of the prophecy of this book."

I, John, am the one who heard and saw these things. And when I heard and saw, I fell down to worship at the feet of the angel who showed me these things. But he said to me, "Do not do that. I am a fellow servant of yours and of your brethren the prophets and of those who heed the words of this book. Worship God."

And he said to me, "Do not seal up the words of the prophecy of this book, for the time is near. Let the one who does wrong, still do wrong; and the one who is filthy, still be filthy; and let the one who is righteous, still practice righteousness; and the one who is holy, still keep himself holy.

Behold, I am coming quickly, and My reward *is* with Me, to render to every man according to what he has done. I am the Alpha and the Omega, the first and the last, the beginning and the end.

Blessed are those who wash their robes, so that they may have the right to the tree of life, and may enter by the gates into the city. Outside are the dogs and the sorcerers and the immoral persons and the murderers and the idolaters, and everyone who loves and practices lying.

I, Jesus, have sent My angel to testify to you these things for the churches. I am the root and the descendant of David, the bright morning star.

The Spirit and the bride say, "Come." And let the one who hears say, "Come." And let the one who is thirsty come; let the one who wishes take the water of life without cost.

I testify to everyone who hears the words of the prophecy of this book: if anyone adds to them, God will add to him the plagues which are written in this book; and if anyone takes away from the words of the book of this prophecy, God will take away his part from the tree of life and from the holy city, which are written in this book.

He who testifies to these things says, "Yes, I am coming quickly." Amen. Come, Lord Jesus.

The grace of the Lord Jesus be with all. Amen. (**REVELATION 22 NASB**)

*Ever since the garden of Eden, when man rebelled against God, we have been cut off from the tree of life (Genesis 3:22–24) and have been subject to death. Here, in this culmination of history, we return to paradise, where there is no death. Until then, may these glimpses into our glorious future comfort and sustain us in our daily lives and challenges.*

# 2

# God's Word in Times of
# Loneliness

Trust me in the depths of your being. It is there that I live in constant communion with you. When you feel flustered and frazzled on the outside, do not get upset with yourself. You are only human, and the swirl of events going on all around you will sometimes feel overwhelming. Rather than scolding yourself for your humanness, remind yourself that I am both with you and within you. I am with you at all times, encouraging and supportive rather than condemning. I know that deep within you, where I live, My Peace is your continual experience.[2]

—*Jesus Calling*

Believers in Jesus are never alone. We may feel lonely, abandoned, and forgotten, but we are not. Sometimes when we feel lonely, we also feel far from God. Though He's but a breath away, we do not approach Him.

Think of the children in the Bible who ran to Jesus—bravely, freely, openly, arms reaching toward Him.

He wanted the children to come to Him even when His disciples tried to keep them away, thinking they would be an annoyance or distraction. He told us that the kingdom of heaven is made up of such as these little ones and that we should come to Him as they do.

But as adults, we try to manage things on our own. We try to keep our needs, hurts, and even our eagerness for comfort in check. We don't want to be a bother or a burden.

How wonderful that He *wants* our burdens, even and especially the ones that are too heavy for us to carry. In 1 Peter 5:6–7, we read, "Therefore humble yourselves under the mighty hand of God, that He may exalt you in due time, *casting all your care upon Him,* for He cares for you" (NKJV).

For a moment, why not be a child again and run to His arms and climb onto His lap? He will pull you up, encircle you with His love, and ease your loneliness as no one else can.

~~~~~~

Behold, I am with you and will keep you wherever you go, and will bring you back to this land; for I will not leave you until I have done what I have spoken to you. (GENESIS 28:15 NKJV)

*God promises Jacob restoration and blessing, renewing the covenant He has made with Israel. Note that He comes to Jacob when he is alone and comfortless. Far from home, he has a long journey to an unknown country ahead and he has the wrath of his brother, Esau, since Jacob had tricked him out of his birthright.*

*But God promises Jacob protection. God never has and never will utterly forsake His people.*

———

The Lord's eyes scan the whole world to find those whose hearts are committed to him and to strengthen them. **(2 CHRONICLES 16:9 GW)**

———

O LORD, You have heard the desire of the humble; You will strengthen their heart, You will incline Your ear. **(PSALM 10:17 NASB)**

———

No one who hopes in you will ever be put to shame, but shame will come on those who are treacherous without cause. Show me your ways, LORD, teach me your paths.

Guide me in your truth and teach me, for you are God my Savior, and my hope is in you all day long.

Remember, LORD, your great mercy and love, for they are from of old. Do not remember the sins of my youth and my rebellious ways; according to your love remember me, for you, LORD, are good.

Good and upright is the LORD; therefore he instructs sinners in his ways. He guides the humble in what is right and teaches them his way. All the ways of the LORD are loving and faithful toward those who keep the demands of his covenant.

For the sake of your name, LORD, forgive my iniquity, though it is great.

Who, then, are those who fear the LORD? He will instruct them in the ways they should choose. They will spend their days in prosperity, and their descendants will inherit the land.

The LORD confides in those who fear him; he makes his covenant known to them. My eyes are ever on the LORD, for only he will release my feet from the snare.

Turn to me and be gracious to me, for I am lonely and afflicted. Relieve the troubles of my heart and free me from my anguish. Look on my affliction and my distress and take away all my sins. (**PSALM 25:3–18 NIV**)

> *This psalm begins and ends with dependence on God. Both new and mature believers need and want to be taught by God. This is the way we can learn to make good decisions and choices as He instructs us. The fear of the Lord is the beginning of wisdom (Psalm 111:10).*

———

God, you are my God. I search for you. I thirst for you like someone in a dry, empty land where there is no water.

I have seen you in the Temple and have seen your strength and glory. Because your love is better than life, I will praise you. I will praise you as long as I live. I will lift up my hands in prayer to your name. I will be content as if I had eaten the best foods. My lips will sing, and my mouth will praise you.

I remember you while I'm lying in bed; I think about you through the night. You are my help. Because of your protection, I sing. I stay close to you; you support me with your right hand. (**PSALM 63:1–8 NCV**)

*It is likely that this psalm was written when David was king and was fleeing for his life from Absalom. More than seeking safety and a refuge from his pursuer, he looks and longs for God, knowing He alone will protect him.*

———

O LORD, You have searched me and known me.
You know when I sit down and when I rise up;
You understand my thought from afar.
You scrutinize my path and my lying down,
And are intimately acquainted with all my ways.
Even before there is a word on my tongue,
Behold, O LORD, You know it all.
You have enclosed me behind and before,
And laid Your hand upon me.
Such knowledge is too wonderful for me;
It is too high, I cannot attain to it.

Where can I go from Your Spirit?
Or where can I flee from Your presence?
If I ascend to heaven, You are there;
If I make my bed in Sheol, behold, You are there.
If I take the wings of the dawn,
If I dwell in the remotest part of the sea,
Even there Your hand will lead me,
And Your right hand will lay hold of me.
If I say, "Surely the darkness will overwhelm me,
And the light around me will be night,"
Even the darkness is not dark to You,

And the night is as bright as the day.
Darkness and light are alike to You.

For You formed my inward parts;
You wove me in my mother's womb.
I will give thanks to You, for I am fearfully and wonderfully made;
Wonderful are Your works,
And my soul knows it very well.
My frame was not hidden from You,
When I was made in secret,
And skillfully wrought in the depths of the earth;
Your eyes have seen my unformed substance;
And in Your book were all written
The days that were ordained for me,
When as yet there was not one of them.

How precious also are Your thoughts to me, O God!
How vast is the sum of them!
If I should count them, they would outnumber the sand.
When I awake, I am still with You.

O that You would slay the wicked, O God;
Depart from me, therefore, men of bloodshed.
For they speak against You wickedly,
And Your enemies take Your name in vain.
Do I not hate those who hate You, O LORD?
And do I not loathe those who rise up against You?
I hate them with the utmost hatred;
They have become my enemies.

Search me, O God, and know my heart;
Try me and know my anxious thoughts;
And see if there be any hurtful way in me,
And lead me in the everlasting way. (**PSALM 139** NASB)

*This psalm emphasizes God's attributes of omnipresence (He is everywhere), omniscience (He knows all), spirituality, infinity (He has no beginning or end) and immutability (He doesn't change). And since He knows all about us, there is no reason to withhold ourselves—our thoughts, needs, and sins—from Him.*

———

The steadfast love of the LORD never ceases; his mercies never come to an end; they are new every morning; great is your faithfulness.

"The LORD is my portion," says my soul, "therefore I will hope in him."

The LORD is good to those who wait for him, to the soul who seeks him. It is good that one should wait quietly for the salvation of the LORD. (**LAMENTATIONS 3:22–26** ESV)

*To "wait quietly" literally means to be in silence, patiently resting in God's will even in times of affliction. God says here that this is a good thing to do. The wonderful hymn "Great Is Thy Faithfulness" reminds us again that every day when we wake up, we can look for new mercies from our loving God, whose faithfulness indeed never ends.*

## —THE COMING MESSIAH—

But you, Bethlehem Ephrathah, though you are little among the thousands of Judah, *yet* out of you shall come forth to Me the One to be Ruler in Israel, whose goings forth *are* from of old, from everlasting.

Therefore He shall give them up, until the time that she who is in labor has given birth; then the remnant of His brethren shall return to the children of Israel.

And He shall stand and feed His flock in the strength of the LORD, in the majesty of the name of the LORD His God; and they shall abide, for now He shall be great to the ends of the earth;

And this One shall be peace. (**MICAH 5:2–5 NKJV**)

*Bethlehem was small and insignificant in size and population, but God chose it as the birthplace of the Messiah. He often uses the little things of the world to outshine the great things in spiritual significance.*

---

The LORD your God is in your midst, a mighty one who will save; he will rejoice over you with gladness; he will quiet you by his love; he will exult over you with loud singing. (**ZEPHANIAH 3:17 ESV**)

*Like a loving human parent, God saves us from calamity, calms us with His love, and rejoices over our very existence. Often this kind of love is too wonderful to be expressed in words. Yet God is so happy with us that He sings—loudly!*

———

And do not fear those who kill the body but cannot kill the soul. Rather fear him who can destroy both soul and body in hell.

Are not two sparrows sold for a penny? And not one of them will fall to the ground apart from your Father.

But even the hairs of your head are all numbered.

Fear not, therefore; you are of more value than many sparrows.

Whoever receives you receives me, and whoever receives me receives him who sent me.

The one who receives a prophet because he is a prophet will receive a prophet's reward, and the one who receives a righteous person because he is a righteous person will receive a righteous person's reward.

And whoever gives one of these little ones even a cup of cold water because he is a disciple, truly, I say to you, he will by no means lose his reward. (**MATTHEW 10:28–31, 40–42** ESV)

*Sometimes we may feel that God is far away and ask, "Where are you, God?" Yet these verses answer that question so that we never have to ask it again. He is right here with us; He misses nothing that happens to us. He notices each sparrow that falls and, much more, what happens to us. If He knows the number of hairs on our heads, surely He also knows and cares when we are lonely or being mistreated.*

———

What man among you, who has 100 sheep and loses one of them, does not leave the 99 in the open field and go after the lost one until he finds it?

When he has found it, he joyfully puts it on his shoulders, and coming home, he calls his friends and neighbors together, saying to them, "Rejoice with me, because I have found my lost sheep!"

I tell you, in the same way, there will be more joy in heaven over one sinner who repents than over 99 righteous people who don't need repentance.

Or what woman who has 10 silver coins, if she loses one coin, does not light a lamp, sweep the house, and search carefully until she finds it? When she finds it, she calls her women friends and neighbors together, saying, "Rejoice with me, because I have found the silver coin I lost!"

I tell you, in the same way, there is joy in the presence of God's angels over one sinner who repents. (LUKE 15:4–10 HCSB)

*If we ever doubt that the individual matters to God, this passage sweeps that doubt away. He knows each of us; He loves each of us; He searches for each of us; and He draws each of us to himself, rejoicing as He does so.*

———

I will ask the Father, and he will give you another Helper to be with you forever—the Spirit of truth. The world cannot accept him, because it does not see him or know him. But you know him, because he lives with you and he will be in you.

I will not leave you all alone like orphans; I will come back to you. In a little while the world will not see me anymore, but you will see me. Because I live, you will live, too.

On that day you will know that I am in my Father, and that you are in me and I am in you.

Those who know my commands and obey them are the ones who love me, and my Father will love those who love me. I will love them and will show myself to them. (**JOHN 14:16–21 NCV**)

*The Holy Spirit is our Comforter, Helper, Advocate, and Guide. Here Jesus emphasizes that it is not only our words, but our actions and commitment that show we love Christ.*

———

For God is not unjust so as to overlook your work and the love that you have shown for his name in serving the saints, as you still do. (**HEBREWS 6:10 ESV**)

———

Behold, I stand at the door and knock. If anyone hears My voice and opens the door, I will come in to him and dine with him, and he with Me. (**REVELATION 3:20 NKJV**)

*Jesus still knocks on the door of our heart, awaiting our response. Notice that He doesn't pulverize the door, knock it down, or make it disappear so He can get in. Ever the gentleman, He waits for us to open the door. Then He promises to come in and eat with us, which indicates intimate fellowship with Him.*

# 3

## God's Word in Times of Illness

As Christians we will sooner or later discover that it is in the valleys of our lives that we find refreshment from God Himself. It is not until we have walked with Him through some very deep troubles that we discover He can lead us to find our refreshment in Him right there in the midst of our difficulty. We are thrilled beyond words when there comes restoration to our souls and spirits from His own gracious spirit.[3]

—*A Shepherd Looks at Psalm 23*

It seems like praise would be the hardest thing in the world to do during difficult times like those of illness. Yet the Bible says we are to give thanks *in* all things (1 Thessalonians 5:18)— not *for* all things, but *in* all circumstances and situations— even when we are sick. We don't have to say, "Thank you for this cancer, God." But we can say, "Thank you for being with me as I go through these treatments" or "I'm thankful, Lord, that my family is helping me during my recuperation."

In every situation there is something to be thankful for. And we can train our minds to look for those things, even in the worst of times.

Once we make that mindset shift from despair and complaint to thanksgiving and praise, things will truly begin to look different. Will we be giddy with happiness about our illnesses or other trials? Of course not. But instead of looking inward in misery, we will start to look upward in thankfulness.

It makes a world of difference.

---

But I have trusted in Your faithful love; my heart will rejoice in Your deliverance. I will sing to the LORD because He has treated me generously. (PSALM 13:5–6 HCSB)

> *Making a list of the good things God has done for us is a helpful exercise. When times are tough, that list can reassure us of God's goodness and faithfulness to us in the past.*

---

KEEP and protect me, O God, for in You I have found refuge, and in You do I put my trust and hide myself. I say to the Lord, You are my Lord; I have no good beside or beyond You.

I will bless the Lord, Who has given me counsel; yes, my heart instructs me in the night seasons. I have set the Lord continually before me; because He is at my right hand, I shall not be moved.

Therefore my heart is glad and my glory [my inner self] rejoices; my body too shall rest and confidently dwell in safety, for You will not abandon me to Sheol (the place of the dead), neither will You suffer Your holy one [Holy One] to see corruption. You will show me the path of life; in Your presence is fullness of joy, at Your right hand there are pleasures forevermore. **(PSALM 16:1–2, 7–11 AMP)**

*When the Lord is at someone's right hand, He is in a position to offer defense or rescue (see Psalm 109:31). The metaphor can mean defense of your body against illness, on the battlefield, or in the courtroom. Your Holy One refers to Christ.*

———

I love you, LORD; you are my strength. The LORD is my rock, my fortress, and my savior; my God is my rock, in whom I find protection. He is my shield, the power that saves me, and my place of safety. **(PSALM 18:1–2 NLT)**

*We can also put on the armor of God described in Ephesians 6:10–17 so that we will be prepared for any battle or trial that comes our way.*

———

I will thank the LORD at all times. My mouth will always praise him. My soul will boast about the LORD. Those who are oppressed will hear it and rejoice.

Praise the LORD's greatness with me. Let us highly honor his name together. I went to the LORD for help. He answered me and rescued me from all my fears.

All who look to him will be radiant. Their faces will never be covered with shame.

Here is a poor man who called out. The LORD heard him and saved him from all his troubles.

The Messenger of the LORD camps around those who fear him, and he rescues them.

Taste and see that the LORD is good. Blessed is the person who takes refuge in him.

Fear the LORD, you holy people who belong to him. Those who fear him are never in need.

Young lions go hungry and may starve, but those who seek the LORD's help have all the good things they need.

Come, children, listen to me. I will teach you the fear of the LORD. Which of you wants a full life? Who would like to live long enough to enjoy good things?

Keep your tongue from saying evil things and your lips from speaking deceitful things. Turn away from evil, and do good. Seek peace, and pursue it!

The LORD's eyes are on righteous people. His ears hear their cry for help.

The LORD confronts those who do evil in order to wipe out all memory of them from the earth.

Righteous people cry out. The LORD hears and rescues them from all their troubles. The LORD is near to those whose hearts are humble. He saves those whose spirits are crushed.

The righteous person has many troubles, but the LORD rescues him from all of them. The LORD guards all of his bones. Not one of them is broken.

Evil will kill wicked people, and those who hate righteous people will be condemned.

The LORD protects the souls of his servants. All who take refuge in him will never be condemned. (PSALM 34 GW)

*The first ten verses are a hymn and the last twelve are a sermon. First, David vows to bless the Lord and urges all to praise Him, sharing his experience with God when He saved him from trouble. Next, he urges us to unwavering faith and obedience, and he ends with teaching about God's faithfulness.*

———

I waited patiently for the LORD; And He inclined to me and heard my cry. He brought me up out of the pit of destruction, out of the miry clay, And He set my feet upon a rock making my footsteps firm. He put a new song in my mouth, a song of praise to our God;

Many will see and fear and will trust in the LORD.

How blessed is the man who has made the LORD his trust, and has not turned to the proud, nor to those who lapse into falsehood. Many, O LORD my God, are the wonders which You have done, and Your thoughts toward us; there is none to compare with You. If I would declare and speak of them, they would be too numerous to count. (PSALM 40:1–5 NASB)

*Hebrews 10:5–9 links this psalm to the Lord Jesus, who waited patiently on His Father throughout His life and torturous death.*

*Without complaining, despairing, or rebelling, He endured it*
*all to accomplish the divine purpose—to save us from our sins.*

———

Oh, send out Your light and Your truth! Let them lead me;
Let them bring me to Your holy hill and to Your tabernacle.
Then I will go to the altar of God, to God my exceeding joy;
and on the harp I will praise You, O God, my God.

Why are you cast down, O my soul? And why are you dis-
quieted within me? Hope in God; for I shall yet praise Him,
the help of my countenance and my God. (**PSALM 43:3–5 NKJV**)

*David knows that the best way to escape one's enemies—whether*
*they are human pursuers or the invisible yet painful enemies of*
*fear, poverty, illness, or broken relationships—is to run to God*
*and rest in His incomparable protection.*

———

Whom have I in heaven but you? And earth has nothing
I desire besides you. My flesh and my heart may fail, but
God is the strength of my heart and my portion forever. (See
**PSALM 73:25–28 NIV**)

———

Turn your ear toward me, O LORD. Answer me, because I
am oppressed and needy. Protect me, because I am faithful
to you. Save your servant who trusts you. You are my God.
Have pity on me, O Lord, because I call out to you all day
long. Give me joy, O Lord, because I lift my soul to you.

You, O Lord, are good and forgiving, full of mercy toward everyone who calls out to you.

Open your ears to my prayer, O LORD. Pay attention when I plead for mercy.

When I am in trouble, I call out to you because you answer me. (**PSALM 86:1–7 GW**)

*Whether our prayers are weak and desperate because of exhaustion or sickness, or joyful and strong because we have experienced a victory, God responds, because He wants us to come to Him with our every need—and every joy. Whether we ask, thank, or praise Him, God wants us to come to Him with boldness.*

---

Those who go to God Most High for safety will be protected by the Almighty. I will say to the LORD, "You are my place of safety and protection. You are my God and I trust you."

God will save you from hidden traps and from deadly diseases. He will cover you with his feathers, and under his wings you can hide. His truth will be your shield and protection. You will not fear any danger by night or an arrow during the day.

You will not be afraid of diseases that come in the dark or sickness that strikes at noon. At your side one thousand people may die, or even ten thousand right beside you, but you will not be hurt. You will only watch and see the wicked punished.

The Lord is your protection; you have made God Most High your place of safety.

Nothing bad will happen to you; no disaster will come to your home.

He has put his angels in charge of you to watch over you wherever you go. They will catch you in their hands so that you will not hit your foot on a rock. You will walk on lions and cobras; you will step on strong lions and snakes.

The Lord says, "Whoever loves me, I will save. I will protect those who know me. They will call to me, and I will answer them. I will be with them in trouble; I will rescue them and honor them. I will give them a long, full life, and they will see how I can save" (PSALM 91 NCV).

*This psalm likely refers to the pestilence mentioned in 2 Samuel 24:13–15. All of the expressions of safety and peace connote the utmost confidence in God. It can be hard for us to remain steadfast in hard times, but this psalm seems to indicate that God is looking for our unwavering love and it does indeed move Him to help us.*

———

All that I am, praise the LORD; everything in me, praise his holy name. My whole being, praise the LORD and do not forget all his kindnesses. He forgives all my sins and heals all my diseases. He saves my life from the grave and loads me with love and mercy. He satisfies me with good things and makes me young again, like the eagle.

The Lord does what is right and fair for all who are wronged by others. He showed his ways to Moses and his deeds to the people of Israel. The LORD shows mercy and is kind. He does not become angry quickly, and he has great love. He will not always accuse us, and he will not be angry forever. He has not punished us as our sins should be punished; he has not repaid us for the evil we have done. As high as the sky is above the earth, so great is his love for those who respect him. He has taken our sins away from us as far as the east is from west. The LORD has mercy on those who respect him, as a father has mercy on his children. He knows how we were made; he remembers that we are dust.

Human life is like grass; we grow like a flower in the field. After the wind blows, the flower is gone, and there is no sign of where it was. But the LORD's love for those who respect him continues forever and ever, and his goodness continues to their grandchildren and to those who keep his agreement and who remember to obey his orders.

The Lord has set his throne in heaven, and his kingdom rules over everything. You who are his angels, praise the LORD. You are the mighty warriors who do what he says and who obey his voice. You, his armies, praise the LORD; you are his servants who do what he wants. Everything the Lord has made should praise him in all the places he rules. My whole being, praise the Lord. (**PSALM 103 NCV**)

*In this beautiful psalm, the psalmist first sings of personal mercies he has received (vv. 1–5); then he extols God's attributes as seen in His dealings with His people (vv. 6–19); and he closes by urging all to join him in praise and adoration of the Lord (vv. 20–22).*

I lift up my eyes to the hills. From where does my help come? My help comes from the LORD, who made heaven and earth.

He will not let your foot be moved; he who keeps you will not slumber. Behold, he who keeps Israel will neither slumber nor sleep.

The LORD is your keeper; the LORD is your shade on your right hand. The sun shall not strike you by day, nor the moon by night.

The LORD will keep you from all evil; he will keep your life. The LORD will keep your going out and your coming in from this time forth and forevermore. (**PSALM 121:1–8 ESV**)

*We might look around at our circumstances in anguish, but when our eyes look up, we find a glimmer of hope. The circumstances might not get better, but hope makes them bearable.*

———

Encourage the exhausted and strengthen the feeble. Say to those with anxious heart, "Take courage, fear not. Behold, your God will come with vengeance; the recompense of God will come, but He will save you" (**ISAIAH 35:3–4 NASB**).

*Often we might feel like the exhausted and feeble, so how can we encourage others? If we reach out, even during our weak times, to comfort another, often our own fear abates and our strength grows.*

———

What can I say now that he has spoken to me? He has done this. I will be careful the rest of my life because of my bitter experience.

Lord, people live in spite of such things, and I have the will to live in spite of them. You give me health and keep me alive. Now my bitter experience turns into peace.

You have saved me and kept me from the rotting pit. You have thrown all my sins behind you.

Sheol doesn't thank you! Death doesn't praise you! Those who go down to the pit cannot expect you to be faithful. Those who are living praise you as I do today.

Fathers make your faithfulness known to their children.

The Lord is going to rescue me, so let us play stringed instruments. We live our lives in the Lord's temple. (**ISAIAH 38:15–20 GW**)

*Life and health are gifts to use in service to God. Here Hezekiah thanks God for restoring him from a time of sickness. Whether or not we are healed physically, as Hezekiah was, we have the assurance that we are His and He will accompany us through all of life's trials and then deliver us to heaven to be with Him.*

———

God is enthroned above the earth, and those who live on it are like grasshoppers. He stretches out the sky like a canopy and spreads it out like a tent to live in. He makes rulers unimportant and makes earthly judges worth nothing. They have hardly been planted. They have hardly been sown. They have hardly taken root in the ground. Then he blows on them and they wither, and a windstorm sweeps them away like straw.

"To whom, then, can you compare me? Who is my equal?" asks the Holy One. Look at the sky and see. Who created these things? Who brings out the stars one by one? He calls them all by name. Because of the greatness of his might and the strength of his power, not one of them is missing.

Jacob, why do you complain? Israel, why do you say, "My way is hidden from the LORD, and my rights are ignored by my God"?

Don't you know? Haven't you heard? The eternal God, the LORD, the Creator of the ends of the earth, doesn't grow tired or become weary. His understanding is beyond reach. He gives strength to those who grow tired and increases the strength of those who are weak.

Even young people grow tired and become weary, and young men will stumble and fall.

Yet, the strength of those who wait with hope in the Lord will be renewed. They will soar on wings like eagles. They will run and won't become weary. They will walk and won't grow tired. (ISAIAH 40:22–40 GW)

———

"My thoughts are not your thoughts, and my ways are not your ways," declares the LORD.

"Just as the heavens are higher than the earth, so my ways are higher than your ways, and my thoughts are higher than your thoughts.

"Rain and snow come down from the sky. They do not go back again until they water the earth. They make it sprout and grow so that it produces seed for farmers and food for people to eat.

"My word, which comes from my mouth, is like the rain and snow. It will not come back to me without results, but it will accomplish whatever I want and achieve whatever I send it to do" (ISAIAH 55:8–11 GW).

> *Other translations of this passage say that God's Word will not come back void or empty and will always produce fruit. This version says that it will not come back without results. When we are too weak, ill, or discouraged even to pray, we can recite God's Word back to Him, knowing that it will do its powerful work no matter how we feel.*

————

And He said to His disciples, "For this reason I say to you, do not worry about your life, as to what you will eat; nor for your body, as to what you will put on. For life is more than food, and the body more than clothing. Consider the ravens, for they neither sow nor reap; they have no storeroom nor barn, and yet God feeds them; how much more valuable you are than the birds! And which of you by worrying can add a single hour to his life's span? If then you cannot do even a very little thing, why do you worry about other matters? Consider the lilies, how they grow: they neither toil nor spin; but I tell you, not even Solomon in all his glory clothed himself like one of these. But if God so clothes the grass in the field, which is alive today and tomorrow is thrown into the furnace, how much more will He clothe you? You men of little faith! And do not seek what you will eat and what you will drink, and do not keep worrying. For all these things the nations of the world eagerly seek; but your Father knows that you need these things. But seek His kingdom, and these things will be added to you. Do not be afraid, little flock, for your Father has chosen gladly to give you the kingdom.

"Sell your possessions and give to charity; make yourselves money belts which do not wear out, an unfailing treasure in heaven, where no thief comes near nor moth destroys. For where your treasure is, there your heart will be also" (**LUKE 12:22–34 NASB**).

*Since God is the author and giver of life, He also is the sustainer of life. Again, as in other verses in the Gospels, we are told to stop all of our hand-wringing, fear, and anxiety for our lives. Having a calm and peaceful demeanor is another way to distinguish the followers of God from those of this world who do not count on Him to provide for them.*

## _ WE ARE AT PEACE WITH GOD _ BECAUSE OF JESUS

Now that we have God's approval because of faith, we have peace with God because of what our Lord Jesus Christ has done. Through Christ we can approach God and stand in his favor. So we brag because of our confidence that we will receive glory from God. But that's not all. We also brag when we are suffering. We know that suffering creates endurance, endurance creates character, and character creates confidence. We're not ashamed to have this confidence, because God's love has been poured into our hearts by the Holy Spirit, who has been given to us.

Look at it this way: At the right time, while we were still helpless, Christ died for ungodly people. Finding someone who would die for a godly person is rare. Maybe someone would have the courage to die for a good person. Christ died for us while we were still sinners. This demonstrates God's love for us.

Since Christ's blood has now given us God's approval, we are even more certain that Christ will save us from God's anger. If the death of his Son restored our relationship with God while we were still his enemies, we are even more certain that, because of this restored relationship, the life his Son lived will save us. In addition, our Lord Jesus Christ lets us continue to brag about God. After all, it is through Christ that we now have this restored relationship with God. (ROMANS 5:1–11 GW)

*We are truly changed when we put our faith in His Son Jesus and thus have peace with God. God cannot have peace with sinners until our sins are forgiven and we are set free of them. We become new people. But brag when we are suffering? Other translations render it glory or boast in our sufferings—because we know that God will use them for good. Again, only through Christ can we do things like this—rejoicing in suffering because we know that God is good.*

Rejoice always, pray continually, give thanks in all circumstances; for this is God's will for you in Christ Jesus. (1 THESSALONIANS 5:16–18 NIV)

———

Brothers and sisters, be patient until the Lord comes again. A farmer patiently waits for his valuable crop to grow from the earth and for it to receive the autumn and spring rains. You, too, must be patient. Do not give up hope, because the Lord is coming soon.

Brothers and sisters, do not complain against each other or you will be judged guilty. And the Judge is ready to come! Brothers and sisters, follow the example of the prophets who spoke for the Lord. They suffered many hard things, but they were patient.

We say they are happy because they did not give up. You have heard about Job's patience, and you know the Lord's purpose for him in the end. You know the Lord is full of mercy and is kind.

My brothers and sisters, above all, do not use an oath when you make a promise. Don't use the name of heaven, earth, or anything else to prove what you say. When you mean yes, say only yes, and when you mean no, say only no so you will not be judged guilty.

Anyone who is having troubles should pray. Anyone who is happy should sing praises. Anyone who is sick should call the church's elders. They should pray for and pour oil on the person in the name of the Lord. And the prayer that is said with faith will make the sick person well; the Lord will heal that person. And if the person has sinned, the sins will be forgiven.

Confess your sins to each other and pray for each other so God can heal you. When a believing person prays, great things happen. (**JAMES 5:7–16 NCV**)

*It's hard to be patient when we are hurting—just stop the pain, please! And yet in this passage we are assured of a blessing if we can endure suffering with patience. Patience means refusing to distrust God, no matter the circumstances.*

# 4

## God's Word in Times of
# Guilt

Guilt is, in fact, one of the oldest sentiments ever expressed in writing, dealt with in the earliest verses of the Bible. After the familiar narrative of the temptation in Genesis 3, we read of Adam and Eve hiding from God's beckoning voice calling, "Where are you?" The question was intended to highlight not so much a place as a condition. Neither Adam nor Eve could break free from the ensuing anguish of choice made in willful violation of God's command.[4]

—*Cries of the Heart*

The hardest person to forgive can be oneself. We may know that God, based on His promises in the Bible and what Jesus did by dying on the cross to pay for our sins, has already forgiven us for all of our sins—past, present, and future. We might believe that in our mind and heart, but we cannot shake the feeling of guilt.

Guilt can be *true* guilt that convicts of us wrongdoing and drives us to God to confess it (or agree with Him that it was wrong) or it can be *false* guilt that results from our taking responsibility for something beyond our control (if I had left just five minutes later that rainy night, I would have avoided the oncoming truck that jumped the median and plowed into my car, killing my infant daughter).

Whether guilt is true or false, it can be crippling if it is not dealt with through God's gracious forgiveness. Let us not be like Adam and Eve and try to hide our sin from God—since He knows all about it anyway. Instead, we can go boldly to Him, knowing that no sin or mistake is too big for Him to handle.

~~~

And the LORD descended in the cloud, and stood with him there, and proclaimed the name of the LORD.

And the LORD passed by before him, and proclaimed, The LORD, The LORD God, merciful and gracious, longsuffering, and abundant in goodness and truth,

Keeping mercy for thousands, forgiving iniquity and transgression and sin, and that will by no means clear the guilty; visiting the iniquity of the fathers upon the children, and upon the children's children, unto the third and to the fourth generation.

And Moses made haste, and bowed his head toward the earth, and worshipped. (**EXODUS 34:5–8 KJV**)

*The Lord is merciful and ready to forgive sin and relieve suffering. He is gracious and kind, lavishing good things on His children. He gives us time to repent and only disciplines when it can help us.*

———

Then the Lord will turn from his fierce anger and be merciful to you. He will have compassion on you and make you a large nation, just as he swore to your ancestors.

The Lord your God will be merciful only if you listen to his voice and keep all his commands that I am giving you today, doing what pleases him. **(DEUTERONOMY 13:17–18 NLT)**

*Here His fierce anger refers to the time in Exodus 32:1–10 where the people made a golden calf while Moses was on Mount Sinai talking to God and receiving the two tablets of commandments written by the finger of God.*

———

Hear the supplication of your servant and of your people Israel when they pray toward this place. Hear from heaven, your dwelling place, and when you hear, forgive. **(1 KINGS 8:30 NIV)**

*Solomon looks to the future for his people, knowing that obedience precedes blessing, and contemplates the continuing need for forgiveness and restoration. The psalmist recalls God's mercy and forgiveness (Psalm 85:2) after his people turned to other gods.*

———

Because your heart was responsive and you humbled yourself before the LORD when you heard what I have spoken against this place and its people—that they would become a curse and be laid waste—and because you tore your robes and wept in my presence, I also have heard you, declares the LORD. (2 KINGS 22:19 NIV)

*A responsive heart here is depicted as one that is soft like wax and able to receive impressions, in contrast with the hard, stony heart that is not moved and does not learn.*

———

If my people who are called by my name humble themselves, and pray and seek my face and turn from their wicked ways, then I will hear from heaven and will forgive their sin and heal their land. (2 CHRONICLES 7:14 ESV)

*God's answer to Solomon's prayer is gracious. His mercy and forgiveness are promised to those who turn to Him.*

———

Nehemiah said, "Go and enjoy choice food and sweet drinks, and send some to those who have nothing prepared. This day is holy to our Lord. Do not grieve, for the joy of the LORD is your strength." (NEHEMIAH 8:10 NIV)

*The public reading of the law, which had not been done for many years, impresses the people with their sin and they experience sorrow over it. Despite their painful memories of their national sin, they are urged to rejoice and be glad.*

———

But you are a forgiving God, gracious and compassionate, slow to anger and abounding in love. Therefore you did not desert them, even when they cast for themselves an image of a calf and said, "This is your god, who brought you up out of Egypt," or when they committed awful blasphemies. (NEHEMIAH 9:17–18 NIV)

*Time and again the Israelites turn from God and forget all the wondrous things He has done for them (see Psalm 78:11). And yet, as He does today, He shows mercy and compassion to His people.*

———

Create in me a pure heart, O God, and renew a steadfast spirit within me. Do not cast me from your presence or take your Holy Spirit from me. Restore to me the joy of your salvation and grant me a willing spirit, to sustain me. (PSALM 51:10–12 NIV)

*This psalm has been called "The Sinner's Guide." Athanasius, a third-century AD believer from Alexandria, Greece, recommended that Christians repeat this prayer when having difficulty sleeping at night.*

———

I am going to gather the people from all the lands where I scattered them in my anger, fury, and terrifying wrath. I will bring them back to this place and make them live here securely. They will be my people, and I will be their God. I will give them the same attitude and the same purpose so that they will fear me as long as they live. This will be for their own good and for the good of their children. I will make an eternal promise to them that I will never stop blessing them. I will make them fear me so that they will never turn away from me. I will enjoy blessing them. With all my heart and soul I will faithfully plant them in this land. (**JEREMIAH 32:37–41 GW**)

> *The word* fear *here means "to give awe, respect, and reverence to God"—He is the only One in the universe who is truly awesome! This passage assures us that He enjoys blessing us for our good. We don't need to be afraid that He will ever decide that He no longer loves us or is fed up with us. Hebrews 13:8 tells us that He is the same yesterday, today, and forever. His is a love that will truly last.*

———

And I will give them one heart [a new heart] and I will put a new spirit within them; and I will take the stony [unnaturally hardened] heart out of their flesh, and will give them a heart of flesh [sensitive and responsive to the touch of their God],

That they may walk in My statutes and keep My ordinances, and do them. And they shall be My people, and I will be their God. (**EZEKIEL 11:19–20 AMP**)

———

And I will give you a new heart, and I will put a new spirit in you. I will take out your stony, stubborn heart and give you a tender, responsive heart. And I will put my Spirit in you so that you will follow my decrees and be careful to obey my regulations. And you will live in Israel, the land I gave your ancestors long ago. You will be my people, and I will be your God. (**EZEKIEL 36:26–28 NLT**)

*These two passages from Ezekiel 11 and 36 are similar in their promise of a new heart and spirit. The stony heart sounds like the stony ground in Matthew 13:5 and 13:20, which cannot receive the good seed. David knew the importance of the heart when he prayed, "Create in me a clean heart, O God; and renew a right spirit within me" (Psalm 51:10 KJV).*

———

Sow righteousness for yourselves and reap faithful love; break up your unplowed ground. It is time to seek the LORD until He comes and sends righteousness on you like the rain. (**HOSEA 10:12 HCSB**)

*The book of Hosea is a beautiful picture of God's love for us—even when we're unfaithful to Him.*

———

Whoever is wise, let him understand these things; whoever is discerning, let him know them; for the ways of the LORD are right, and the upright walk in them, but transgressors stumble in them. (**HOSEA 14:9 ESV**)

*Hosea summarizes his teaching here. Jesus is a foundation stone to some and a stone of stumbling and a rock of offense to others. The stone of stumbling and rock of offense are also mentioned in Isaiah 8:14, Romans 9:32–33, and 1 Peter 2:8.*

## —THE COMING DAY OF JUDGMENT—

The LORD of Heaven's Armies says, "The day of judgment is coming, burning like a furnace. On that day the arrogant and the wicked will be burned up like straw. They will be consumed—roots, branches, and all.

"But for you who fear my name, the Sun of Righteousness will rise with healing in his wings. And you will go free, leaping with joy like calves let out to pasture. On the day when I act, you will tread upon the wicked as if they were dust under your feet," says the LORD of Heaven's Armies. (**MALACHI 4:1–3 NLT**)

*This passage predicts the coming judgment of the wicked and the happiness of the righteous. But each of us knows that we aren't righteous at all. We're just human. How comforting to know that when God looks at us, He sees us through the righteousness of Jesus so that we are clothed with His righteousness (Isaiah 61:10).*

———

Pray, then, in this way:
"Our Father who is in heaven,
Hallowed be Your name.
Your kingdom come.
Your will be done, on earth as it is in heaven.
Give us this day our daily bread.
And forgive us our debts, as we also have forgiven our debtors.

And do not lead us into temptation, but deliver us from evil.

For Yours is the kingdom and the power and the glory forever. Amen" (**MATTHEW 6:9–13 NASB**).

## —THE PARABLE OF THE LOST SON—

A certain man had two sons. And the younger of them said to *his* father, "Father, give me the portion of goods that falls *to me.*" So he divided to them *his* livelihood.

And not many days after, the younger son gathered all together, journeyed to a far country, and there wasted his possessions with prodigal living.

But when he had spent all, there arose a severe famine in that land, and he began to be in want.

Then he went and joined himself to a citizen of that country, and he sent him into his fields to feed swine. And he would gladly have filled his stomach with the pods that the swine ate, and no one gave him anything.

But when he came to himself, he said, "How many of my father's hired servants have bread enough and to spare, and I perish with hunger!

"I will arise and go to my father, and will say to him, 'Father, I have sinned against heaven and before you, and I am no longer worthy to be called your son. Make me like one of your hired servants.' "

And he arose and came to his father. But when he was still a great way off, his father saw him and had compassion, and ran and fell on his neck and kissed him.

And the son said to him, "Father, I have sinned against heaven and in your sight, and am no longer worthy to be called your son."

But the father said to his servants, "Bring out the best robe and put it on him, and put a ring on his hand and sandals on his feet.

"And bring the fatted calf here and kill it, and let us eat and be merry; for this my son was dead and is alive again; he was lost and is found." And they began to be merry. (**LUKE 15:11–24** NKJV)

*The story of the prodigal son is a favorite because we all know that we have strayed from our Father and engaged in some prodigal living apart from Him. Yet we see in this marvelous passage that when we return to Him, we do not get rejection and judgment, but instead He welcomes us with open arms. What a Father!*

For God so loved the world that He gave His only begotten Son, that whoever believes in Him should not perish but have everlasting life. For God did not send His Son into the world to condemn the world, but that the world through Him might be saved.

He who believes in Him is not condemned; but he who does not believe is condemned already, because he has not believed in the name of the only begotten Son of God. (**JOHN 3:16–18** NKJV)

*Can you imagine giving your only son for people you knew would reject and scorn Him? Of course we cannot. That takes love far beyond human ability to even imagine. But this amazing sacrifice is the only evidence we need of His unfathomable love toward us. "But God commendeth his love toward us, in that, while we were yet sinners, Christ died for us" (Romans 5:8 KJV).*

---

So Jesus said to the Jews who believed in him, "If you continue to obey my teaching, you are truly my followers. Then you will know the truth, and the truth will make you free" (**JOHN 8:31–32 NCV**).

---

So now, those who are in Christ Jesus are not judged guilty. Through Christ Jesus the law of the Spirit that brings life made you free from the law that brings sin and death. (**ROMANS 8:1–2 NCV**)

*Although believers may suffer, we will not be condemned with the world (those outside of Christ). This is true freedom, knowing that God will save us, His children.*

---

If you confess with your mouth Jesus as Lord, and believe in your heart that God raised Him from the dead, you will be saved; for with the heart a person believes, resulting in righteousness, and with the mouth he confesses, resulting in salvation.

For the Scripture says, "WHOEVER BELIEVES IN HIM WILL NOT BE DISAPPOINTED." For there is no distinction between Jew and Greek; for the same Lord is Lord of all, abounding in riches for all who call on Him; for "WHOEVER WILL CALL ON THE NAME OF THE LORD WILL BE SAVED" (**ROMANS 10:9–13 NASB**).

*What a promise! And it is the same promise to all who call on God, believing on Him for salvation. You don't have to be of a certain group or church or ethnicity or country or background— He wants us all!*

---

No temptation has overtaken you but such as is common to man; and God is faithful, who will not allow you to be tempted beyond what you are able, but with the temptation will provide the way of escape also, that you may be able to endure it. (**1 CORINTHIANS 10:13 NASB**)

*Temptation isn't sin. Even Jesus was tempted by the devil in the desert. Sin is the giving in to the temptation. And this verse promises us that God will help us to flee from temptation so that we do not sin. Of course, even when we do, He is there ready and waiting to forgive and restore us to himself.*

---

But because of his great love for us, God, who is rich in mercy, made us alive with Christ even when we were dead in transgressions—it is by grace you have been saved. And God raised us up with Christ and seated us with him in the heavenly realms in Christ Jesus, in order that in the coming ages he might show the incomparable riches of his grace, expressed in his kindness to us in Christ Jesus. For it is by grace you have been saved, through faith—and this is not from yourselves, it is the gift of God—not by works, so that no one can boast. For we are God's handiwork, created in Christ Jesus to do good works, which God prepared in advance for us to do. (**EPHESIANS 2:4–10 NIV**)

*What good news—no matter how hard we try, we cannot earn salvation by working for it. It is purely a gift from our loving God. Picture a lifeless figure dead at the side of the road and the merciful Messiah comes along, picks him up, restores him to life, and takes him with Him. We were dead in our sins, but even so, God raised us up and forgave us, making us new again.*

Yes, everything else is worthless when compared with the infinite value of knowing Christ Jesus my Lord. For his sake I have discarded everything else, counting it all as garbage, so that I could gain Christ and become one with him. I no longer count on my own righteousness through obeying the law; rather, I become righteous through faith in Christ. For God's way of making us right with himself depends on faith. I want to know Christ and experience the mighty power that raised him from the dead. I want to suffer with him, sharing in his death, so that one way or another I will experience the resurrection from the dead!

I don't mean to say that I have already achieved these things or that I have already reached perfection. But I press on to possess that perfection for which Christ Jesus first possessed me. No, dear brothers and sisters, I have not achieved it, but I focus on this one thing: Forgetting the past and looking forward to what lies ahead, I press on to reach the end of the race and receive the heavenly prize for which God, through Christ Jesus, is calling us. (**PHILIPPIANS 3:8–14 NLT**)

*Paul emphasizes the effort involved in living the victorious life. Running a race requires preparation, discipline, and persever-ance. It isn't easy. But he looks forward to the prize God has for him and for us at the end of the race. Notice how he doesn't look back or get bogged down in past mistakes or regrets. "Forgetting the past and looking forward to what lies ahead" is often exactly what we need to do.*

———

Now to Him who is able to keep you from stumbling, and to make you stand in the presence of His glory blameless with great joy, to the only God our Savior, through Jesus Christ our Lord, be glory, majesty, dominion and authority, before all time and now and forever. Amen. (**JUDE 24–25 NASB**)

———

But you have a few there in Sardis who have kept their clothes unstained, so they will walk with me and will wear white clothes, because they are worthy. Those who win the victory will be dressed in white clothes like them. And I will not erase their names from the book of life, but I will say they belong to me before my Father and before his angels. Everyone who has ears should listen to what the Spirit says to the churches. (**REVELATION 3:4–6 NCV**)

*Even in a corrupt and wicked culture, some still trust God and Christ's righteousness covers them. But they can become defiled by sinful activities. By confessing their sins, they can stay in close fellowship with God (see 1 John 1:9).*

# 5

## God's Word in Times of
# Persecution

Interestingly, Paul wrote several letters during those years of house arrest, one of which was addressed to a group of Christians living in Philippi. It is an amazing letter, made even more remarkable by its recurring theme—joy. Think of it! Written by a man who had known excruciating hardship and pain, living in a restricted setting chained to a Roman soldier, the letter to the Philippians resounds with joy! Attitudes of joy and contentment are woven through the tapestry of these 104 verses like threads of silver. Rather than wallowing in self-pity or calling on his friends to help him escape or at least find relief from these restrictions, Paul sent a surprisingly lighthearted message. And on top of all that, time and again he urges the Philippians (and his readers) to be people of joy.[5]

—*Laugh Again*

Joy and suffering seem to be opposites. And yet we read in James 1:2–3, "Count it all joy, my brothers, when you meet trials of various kinds, for you know that the testing of your faith produces steadfastness" (ESV).

That doesn't mean that suffering is "fun" or enjoyable. Paul, who had persecuted Christians for their faith, was now being persecuted for *his* faith. His imprisonment clearly wasn't fun. It was painful and very difficult. Our suffering, too, can be excruciating, and we don't want to minimize it or take it lightly.

But isn't it comforting to know that behind our suffering, God is doing something good? He is producing "steadfastness" in us. To be steadfast is to be firmly fixed in place; firm in belief, determination, or adherence; loyal, not subject to change; faithful. In addition to building our strength and determination, suffering gives us an opportunity to honor Jesus by imitating Him, who for the joy that was set before Him endured the cross, despising the shame, and is seated at the right hand of the throne of God (from Hebrews 12:2). His was the ultimate persecution.

While it is unlikely that we are *happy* during times of trial, we can still know that settled state of mind and heart that gives us confidence and hope—*joy*.

<hr />

"As for you, you meant evil against me, *but* God meant it for good in order to bring about this present result, to preserve many people alive. So therefore, do not be afraid; I will provide for you and your little ones." So he comforted them and spoke kindly to them. (**GENESIS 50:20–21 NASB**)

> *Many years earlier, Joseph's brothers had sold him into slavery because they were jealous of him (see Genesis 37:26–27). Now his brothers must face him to ask for grain during a famine. His gracious response—returning good for evil—shows his complete faith in God and certainty about His goodness.*

———

As Pharaoh approached, the Israelites looked up and saw that the Egyptians were coming after them. Terrified, the Israelites cried out to the LORD. They said to Moses, "Did you bring us out into the desert to die because there were no graves in Egypt? Look what you've done by bringing us out of Egypt! Didn't we tell you in Egypt, 'Leave us alone! Let us go on serving the Egyptians'? It would have been better for us to serve the Egyptians than to die in the desert!"

Moses answered the people, "Don't be afraid! Stand still, and see what the Lord will do to save you today. You will never see these Egyptians again. The Lord is fighting for you! So be still!"

Then the LORD said to Moses, "Why are you crying out to me? Tell the Israelites to start moving. Raise your staff, stretch out your hand over the sea, and divide the water. Then the Israelites will go through the sea on dry ground. I am making the Egyptians so stubborn that they will follow the Israelites. I will receive honor because of what I will do to Pharaoh, his entire army, his chariots, and cavalry. The Egyptians will know that I am the LORD when I am honored for what I did to Pharaoh, his chariots, and his cavalry."

The Messenger of God, who had been in front of the Israelites, moved behind them. So the column of smoke moved from in front of the Israelites and stood behind them between the Egyptian camp and the Israelite camp. The column of smoke was there when darkness came, and it lit up the night. Neither side came near the other all night long.

Then Moses stretched out his hand over the sea. All that night the LORD pushed back the sea with a strong east wind and turned the sea into dry ground. The water divided, and the Israelites went through the middle of the sea on dry ground. The water stood like a wall on their right and on their left.

The Egyptians pursued them, and all Pharaoh's horses, chariots, and cavalry followed them into the sea. Just before dawn, the LORD looked down from the column of fire and smoke and threw the Egyptian camp into a panic. He made the wheels of their chariots come off so that they could hardly move. Then the Egyptians shouted, "Let's get out of here! The LORD is fighting for Israel! He's against us!" (EXODUS 14:10–25 GW).

*In recounting God's goodness to the Israelites, the psalmist refers to this occasion in Psalm 106:8–10, "He saved them because of his reputation so that he could make his mighty power known. He angrily commanded the Red Sea, and it dried up. He led them through deep water as though it were a desert. He rescued them from the power of the one who hated them. He rescued them from the enemy."*

*Be still. The Lord is fighting for you. What a great encouragement to know that God has every situation under control.*

---

Many say, Oh, that we might see some good! Lift up the light of Your countenance upon us, O Lord. You have put more joy and rejoicing in my heart than [they know] when their wheat and new wine have yielded abundantly. In peace I will both lie down and sleep, for You, Lord, alone make me dwell in safety and confident trust. (**PSALM 4:6–8 AMP**)

*Difficulty sleeping often is a symptom of worry, anxiety, and fear. Yet David, surrounded by enemies, possesses the peace that passes all understanding that allows him to rest, trusting in God.*

---

The LORD is a shelter for the oppressed, a refuge in times of trouble. Those who know your name trust in you, for you, O LORD, do not abandon those who search for you. (**PSALM 9:9–10 NLT**)

*In times of trouble, we need a refuge, a place to go where we can be safe. This wonderful promise is for those who search for God, and as Jeremiah 29:13 says, "You will seek me and find me when you seek me with all your heart" (NIV).*

---

But I will call on God, and the LORD will rescue me. Morning, noon, and night I cry out in my distress, and the LORD hears my voice. He ransoms me and keeps me safe from the battle waged against me, though many still oppose me. God, who has ruled forever, will hear me and humble them. Give your burdens to the LORD, and he will take care of you. (PSALM 55:16–19, 22 NLT)

*Instead of plotting against his adversaries, the psalmist turns to God. Jesus did this also, and every Christian would be wise to do the same. The more desperate the times, the more tightly we must cling to God.*

———

In God, whose word I praise, in the LORD, whose word I praise—in God I trust and am not afraid. What can man do to me?

I am under vows to you, my God; I will present my thank offerings to you. For you have delivered me from death and my feet from stumbling, that I may walk before God in the light of life. (PSALM 56:10–13 NIV)

*It is even by God's grace and enablement that we are able to praise Him—just like it's only because He draws us to himself and gives us the gift of faith that we are able to believe. So whether we are experiencing good times or difficulties, we must remember that the ability to persist and endure are from Him who deserves our praise in every situation.*

———

I called on the LORD in distress; the LORD answered me and set me in a broad place. The LORD is on my side; I will not fear. What can man do to me? The LORD is for me among those who help me; therefore I shall see my desire on those who hate me. It is better to trust in the LORD than to put confidence in man. It is better to trust in the LORD than to put confidence in princes. (**PSALM 118:5–9 NKJV**)

## BIRTH AND REIGN
## OF THE PRINCE OF PEACE

But there will be no more gloom for her who was in anguish; in earlier times He treated the land of Zebulun and the land of Naphtali with contempt, but later on He shall make it glorious, by the way of the sea, on the other side of Jordan, Galilee of the Gentiles.

The people who walk in darkness will see a great light; those who live in a dark land, the light will shine on them.

You shall multiply the nation, You shall increase their gladness; they will be glad in Your presence as with the gladness of harvest, as men rejoice when they divide the spoil.

For You shall break the yoke of their burden and the staff on their shoulders, the rod of their oppressor, as at the battle of Midian. For every boot of the booted warrior in the battle tumult, and cloak rolled in blood, will be for burning, fuel for the fire.

For a child will be born to us, a son will be given to us; and the government will rest on His shoulders; and His name will be called Wonderful Counselor, Mighty God, Eternal Father, Prince of Peace.

There will be no end to the increase of His government or of peace, on the throne of David and over his kingdom, to establish it and to uphold it with justice and righteousness from then on and forevermore.

The zeal of the LORD of hosts will accomplish this. (ISAIAH 9:1–7 NASB)

*When the gospel comes to any place or person, light comes with it. The gospel brings joy. The Jews were delivered from the yoke of many oppressors, foreshadowing the believer's deliverance from sin by the Messiah, the Wonderful Counselor, Mighty God, Eternal Father, Prince of Peace. The Child would be born for the benefit of all sinners, all believers from the beginning to the end of the world.*

———

Daniel said, "Let the name of God be blessed forever and ever, for wisdom and power belong to Him.

"It is He who changes the times and the epochs; He removes kings and establishes kings; He gives wisdom to wise men and knowledge to men of understanding.

"It is He who reveals the profound and hidden things; He knows what is in the darkness, and the light dwells with Him.

"To You, O God of my fathers, I give thanks and praise, for You have given me wisdom and power; even now You have made known to me what we requested of You, for You have made known to us the king's matter." (DANIEL 2:20–23 NASB)

*God had revealed the meaning of King Nebuchadnezzar's dream to Daniel, sparing the lives of Daniel and all the other wise men in the kingdom. When Daniel told the king the meaning of the dream, he gave God the credit, saying, "There is a God in heaven who reveals mysteries, and He has made known to*

*King Nebuchadnezzar what will take place in the latter days"*
*(Daniel 2:28 NASB).*

———

It has seemed good to me to declare the signs and wonders which the Most High God has done for me.

How great are His signs and how mighty are His wonders! His kingdom is an everlasting kingdom and His dominion is from generation to generation. (**DANIEL 4:2–3 NASB**)

*Even the arrogant King Nebuchadnezzar, who had ordered Daniel's friends Shadrach, Meshach, and Abednego to be thrown into the fiery furnace, acknowledged God's power and goodness after God saved the three men from death.*

———

But as for me, I will watch expectantly for the LORD; I will wait for the God of my salvation. My God will hear me.

Do not rejoice over me, O my enemy. Though I fall I will rise; though I dwell in darkness, the LORD is a light for me. (**MICAH 7:7–8 NASB**)

## —JESUS PRAYS FOR HIS FOLLOWERS—

After Jesus said these things, he looked toward heaven and prayed, "Father, the time has come. Give glory to your Son so that the Son can give glory to you.

You gave the Son power over all people so that the Son could give eternal life to all those you gave him.

And this is eternal life: that people know you, the only true God, and that they know Jesus Christ, the One you sent.

Having finished the work you gave me to do, I brought you glory on earth. And now, Father, give me glory with you; give me the glory I had with you before the world was made.

I showed what you are like to those you gave me from the world. They belonged to you, and you gave them to me, and they have obeyed your teaching. Now they know that everything you gave me comes from you.

I gave them the teachings you gave me, and they accepted them. They knew that I truly came from you, and they believed that you sent me.

I am praying for them. I am not praying for people in the world but for those you gave me, because they are yours. All I have is yours, and all you have is mine. And my glory is shown through them.

I am coming to you; I will not stay in the world any longer. But they are still in the world. Holy Father, keep them safe by the power of your name, the name you gave me, so that they will be one, just as you and I are one.

While I was with them, I kept them safe by the power of your name, the name you gave me. I protected them, and only one of them, the one worthy of destruction, was lost so that the Scripture would come true.

I am coming to you now. But I pray these things while I am still in the world so that these followers can have all of my joy in them. I have given them your teaching. And the world has hated them, because they don't belong to the world, just as I don't belong to the world.

I am not asking you to take them out of the world but to keep them safe from the Evil One. They don't belong to the world, just as I don't belong to the world. Make them ready for your service through your truth; your teaching is truth.

I have sent them into the world, just as you sent me into the world. For their sake, I am making myself ready to serve so that they can be ready for their service of the truth.

I pray for these followers, but I am also praying for all those who will believe in me because of their teaching.

Father, I pray that they can be one. As you are in me and I am in you, I pray that they can also be one in us. Then the world will believe that you sent me. I have given these people the glory that you gave me so that they can be one, just as you and I are one. I will be in them and you will be in me so that they will be completely one. Then the world will know that you sent me and that you loved them just as much as you loved me.

Father, I want these people that you gave me to be with me where I am. I want them to see my glory, which you gave me because you loved me before the world was made. Father, you are the One who is good. The world does not know you, but I know you, and these people know you sent me. I showed them what you are like, and I will show them again. Then they will have the same love that you have for me, and I will live in them" (JOHN 17 NCV).

*This is Jesus' great intercessory prayer for His followers. He asks the Father to complete what the Son has begun in them. He asks for unity among believers and joy as they serve Him and face trials, persecutions, and suffering, knowing that God's hand is on everything they experience.*

———

We are hard pressed on every side, but not crushed; perplexed, but not in despair; persecuted, but not abandoned; struck down, but not destroyed. We always carry around in our body the death of Jesus, so that the life of Jesus may also be revealed in our body.

Therefore we do not lose heart. Though outwardly we are wasting away, yet inwardly we are being renewed day by day. For our light and momentary troubles are achieving for us an eternal glory that far outweighs them all. So we fix our eyes not on what is seen, but on what is unseen, since what is seen is temporary, but what is unseen is eternal. (**2 CORINTHIANS 4:8–10, 16–18 NIV**)

> *In times of desperation, this passage can really strengthen us because it bolsters us with courage—we are hard pressed, perplexed, persecuted, and struck down. And yet we can bear it because God promises that we won't lose heart or be crushed, despairing, abandoned, or destroyed. He has our backs.*

———

Finally, be strong in the Lord and in his mighty power. Put on the full armor of God, so that you can take your stand against the devil's schemes. For our struggle is not against flesh and blood, but against the rulers, against the authorities, against the powers of this dark world and against the spiritual forces of evil in the heavenly realms. Therefore put on the full armor of God, so that when the day of evil comes, you may be able to stand your ground, and after you have done everything, to stand. Stand firm then, with the belt of truth buckled around your waist, with the breastplate of righteousness in place, and with your feet fitted with the readiness that comes from the gospel of peace. In addition to all this, take up the shield of faith, with which you can extinguish all the flaming arrows of the evil one. Take the helmet of salvation and the sword of the Spirit, which is the word of God.

And pray in the Spirit on all occasions with all kinds of prayers and requests. With this in mind, be alert and always keep on praying for all the Lord's people. (**EPHESIANS 6:10–18** **ESV**)

> *This is Paul's final admonition to the church at Ephesus. They are engaged in fierce spiritual warfare and they need weapons and equipment with which to fight. Like them, once we are equipped with the armor of God, we must stand firm, knowing that the battle has already been won for us.*

Rejoice in the Lord always. I will say it again: Rejoice!

Let your gentleness be evident to all. The Lord is near. Do not be anxious about anything, but in every situation, by prayer and petition, with thanksgiving, present your requests to God. And the peace of God, which transcends all understanding, will guard your hearts and your minds in Christ Jesus.

Finally, brothers and sisters, whatever is true, whatever is noble, whatever is right, whatever is pure, whatever is lovely, whatever is admirable—if anything is excellent or praisewor-thy—think about such things. Whatever you have learned or received or heard from me, or seen in me—put it into practice. And the God of peace will be with you.

I rejoiced greatly in the Lord that at last you renewed your concern for me. Indeed, you were concerned, but you had no opportunity to show it.

I am not saying this because I am in need, for I have learned to be content whatever the circumstances. I know what it is to be in need, and I know what it is to have plenty. I have learned the secret of being content in any and every situation, whether well fed or hungry, whether living in plenty or in want.

I can do all this through him who gives me strength. (PHILIPPIANS 4:4–13 NIV)

*Here Paul is a prisoner, who would soon be tried for his life. It is hard to comprehend how he could be rejoicing and urging others to do so in such a situation. Only as we understand what he fixed his mind on—what is true, noble, right, pure, lovely, admirable, excellent, praiseworthy—can we begin to imagine such a victory. Measuring our thoughts against that list will help us toss out a great many that do not fit the criteria Paul provides and certainly do not add to our peace.*

———

Every Scripture is God-breathed (given by His inspiration) and profitable for instruction, for reproof and conviction of sin, for correction of error and discipline in obedience, [and] for training in righteousness (in holy living, in confor-mity to God's will in thought, purpose, and action), so that the man of God may be complete and proficient, well fitted and thoroughly equipped for every good work. (2 TIMOTHY 3:16–17 AMP)

> *The Bible equips us for life and service to God and also for with-standing adversity. God's Word is the sword of the spirit described in Ephesians 6 along with the rest of the armor of God. When Paul wrote this, only a part of the New Testament was written. How much more equipped are we with both the Old and New Testaments at our disposal.*

———

Blessed is the man that endureth temptation: for when he is tried, he shall receive the crown of life, which the Lord hath promised to them that love him. (JAMES 1:12 KJV)

———

Beloved, do not think it strange concerning the fiery trial which is to try you, as though some strange thing happened to you; but rejoice to the extent that you partake of Christ's sufferings, that when His glory is revealed, you may also be glad with exceeding joy.

If you are reproached for the name of Christ, blessed are you, for the Spirit of glory and of God rests upon you. On their part He is blasphemed, but on your part He is glorified. (1 PETER 4:12–14 NKJV)

> *If we are persecuted, criticized, mocked, or vilified for the name of Christ, we are sharing in His suffering and will also share in His glory. And we don't go through it alone, for the Holy Spirit is with us during every moment of every trial.*

Behold, He is coming with the clouds, and every eye will see Him, even those who pierced Him; and all the tribes of the earth shall gaze upon Him and beat their breasts and mourn and lament over Him. Even so [must it be]. Amen (so be it).

I am the Alpha and the Omega, the Beginning and the End, says the Lord God, He Who is and Who was and Who is to come, the Almighty (the Ruler of all). (**REVELATION 1:7–8 AMP**)

*Revelation has two main parts, given to John by the Lord: the state of the church at the time, including the letters of John to the seven churches, and the appearance of the Lord Jesus. The letters to the churches contain precepts, promises, and warnings applicable to churches of all times, including today. John is a prisoner on this rocky island, being persecuted for his faith.*

Then there was a war in heaven. Michael and his angels fought against the dragon, and the dragon and his angels fought back. But the dragon was not strong enough, and he and his angels lost their place in heaven. The giant dragon was thrown down out of heaven. (He is that old snake called the devil or Satan, who tricks the whole world.) The dragon with his angels was thrown down to the earth.

Then I heard a loud voice in heaven saying: "The salvation and the power and the kingdom of our God and the authority of his Christ have now come. The accuser of our brothers and sisters, who accused them day and night before our God, has been thrown down.

"And our brothers and sisters defeated him by the blood of the Lamb's death and by the message they preached. They did not love their lives so much that they were afraid of death.

"So rejoice, you heavens and all who live there! But it will be terrible for the earth and the sea, because the devil has come down to you! He is filled with anger, because he knows he does not have much time" (REVELATION 12:7–12 NCV).

*This passage is symbolic of the casting down of Satan, who has tried to destroy Christians throughout history. The heroism of the lives and deaths of the believers puts fear into the hearts of the enemies of God. Satan will try once again, but we are assured that the ultimate victory is Christ's.*

———

This means that God's holy people must endure persecution patiently, obeying his commands and maintaining their faith in Jesus.

And I heard a voice from heaven saying, "Write this down: Blessed are those who die in the Lord from now on. Yes, says the Spirit, they are blessed indeed, for they will rest from their hard work; for their good deeds follow them!"

Then I saw a white cloud, and seated on the cloud was someone like the Son of Man. He had a gold crown on his head and a sharp sickle in his hand. (REVELATION 14:12–14 NLT)

*We are exhorted again to persevere during persecution and suf-*
*fering, knowing that the reward for doing so will be great. Jesus*
*said that the Son of man will be seen coming on the clouds of*
*heaven and will send his angels to gather the believers (Mat-*
*thew 24:30–31). Here John sees the Son of man sitting upon*
*a white cloud.*

———

Then I saw another sign in heaven, great and marvelous: seven
angels having the seven last plagues, for in them the wrath
of God is complete.

And I saw something like a sea of glass mingled with fire,
and those who have the victory over the beast, over his image
and over his mark and over the number of his name, standing
on the sea of glass, having harps of God. They sing the song of
Moses, the servant of God, and the song of the Lamb, saying:

"Great and marvelous are Your works, Lord God Al-
mighty! Just and true *are* Your ways, O King of the saints!
Who shall not fear You, O Lord, and glorify Your name?
For You alone are holy. For all nations shall come and wor-
ship before You, for Your judgments have been manifested"
**(REVELATION 15:1–4 NKJV).**

*This chapter describes the closing judgments upon "the beast*
*and its image or for anyone who receives the mark of its name"*
*(14:11 NIV). The sea of glass mingled with fire symbolizes the*
*purity and calmness of God's rule and the judgment indicated*
*by the fire. The redeemed sing of deliverance and praise. They*
*who have experienced persecution from the beast rejoice because*
*its judgment has come.*

And the twenty-four elders and the four living creatures fell down and worshiped God who was seated on the throne, saying, "Amen. Hallelujah!" And from the throne came a voice saying,

"Praise our God, all you his servants, you who fear him, small and great."

Then I heard what seemed to be the voice of a great multitude, like the roar of many waters and like the sound of mighty peals of thunder, crying out,

"Hallelujah! For the Lord our God the Almighty reigns. Let us rejoice and exult and give him the glory, for the marriage of the Lamb has come, and his Bride has made herself ready; it was granted her to clothe herself with fine linen, bright and pure"—for the fine linen is the righteous deeds of the saints.

And the angel said to me, "Write this: Blessed are those who are invited to the marriage supper of the Lamb." And he said to me, "These are the true words of God."

Then I fell down at his feet to worship him, but he said to me, "You must not do that! I am a fellow servant with you and your brothers who hold to the testimony of Jesus. Worship God." For the testimony of Jesus is the spirit of prophecy.

Then I saw heaven opened, and behold, a white horse! The one sitting on it is called Faithful and True, and in righteousness he judges and makes war. His eyes are like a flame of fire, and on his head are many diadems, and he has a name written that no one knows but himself. He is clothed in a robe dipped in blood, and the name by which he is called is The Word of God. And the armies of heaven, arrayed in fine linen, white and pure, were following him on white horses. From his mouth comes a sharp sword with which to strike down the nations, and he will rule them with a rod of iron. He will tread the winepress of the fury of the wrath of God the Almighty. On his robe and on his thigh he has a name written, King of kings and Lord of lords.

Then I saw an angel standing in the sun, and with a loud voice he called to all the birds that fly directly overhead, "Come, gather for the great supper of God, to eat the flesh of kings, the flesh of captains, the flesh of mighty men, the flesh of horses and their riders, and the flesh of all men, both free and slave, both small and great." And I saw the beast and the kings of the earth with their armies gathered to make war against him who was sitting on the horse and against his army. And the beast was captured, and with it the false prophet who in its presence had done the signs by which he deceived those who had received the mark of the beast and those who worshiped its image. These two were thrown alive into the lake of fire that burns with sulfur. And the rest were slain by the sword that came from the mouth of him who was sitting on the horse, and all the birds were gorged with their flesh. (**REVELATION 19:4–21 ESV**)

> *It's hard to imagine the thrill of being part of this throng praising God because Christ is the victor. Of note is the angel's admonition to John not to bow down in worship before him, but only before*

God. Some confuse the Creator with His creation. Angels are created beings, like we are. They are not to be worshiped, prayed to, or bowed down before. Those who believed Satan's lies instead of God's truth "worshiped and served the creature rather than the Creator" (Romans 1:25 NASB).

# 6

# God's Word in Times of **Failure** or **Unmet** Expectations

While it's natural to continue seeking solutions to our challenges, it's unrealistic to expect that all our challenges will resolve the way we want them to. Theologian Terry Muck has said the difference between city dwellers and farmers is that city dwellers expect every year to be better than the previous year. If they don't get a raise, buy something new, or end up better off, they think they are failures. Farmers don't see it that way. They know there will be good years and bad years; they know they can't control the weather or prevent a bad crop. So they learn to work hard and accept what comes.[6]

*—When the Bottom Drops Out*

Disappointment—it is universally experienced and universally disliked. Yet Erwin Lutzer, pastor of Moody Church in Chicago, said that disappointment is caused by having a wrong focus. People, being human, will let us down. Jobs, as we know, can end suddenly. Health is subject to change. Financial security turns out to be anything but secure.

But God never changes. He is the same yesterday, today, and tomorrow. He promises to use all things that happen to those of us who love Him—even failure, even letdowns and disappointment—for good and for His purposes.

Does that mean that we simply pretend that we are never disappointed and assure ourselves and others that being a Christian means plastering a smile on your face at all times, no matter what you're going through?

No. It means that we can start to think like farmers—we know we can't control everything and we will experience both happiness and disappointment. In light of that, we will work hard and accept what comes.

<hr />

I have come down to rescue them from the power of the Egyptians and to bring them from that land to a good and spacious land, a land flowing with milk and honey—the territory of the Canaanites, Hittites, Amorites, Perizzites, Hivites, and Jebusites. The Israelites' cry for help has come to Me, and I have also seen the way the Egyptians are oppressing them. Therefore, go. I am sending you to Pharaoh so that you may lead My people, the Israelites, out of Egypt.
(EXODUS 3:8–10 HCSB)

*"Milk and honey" refers to the bounty of the land. Canaan was rich in natural resources and in cultivated produce. God heard the Israelites' cry and planned to lead them out of slavery and into fertile land. He still hears the cries of His children today and helps them.*

———

Then Hannah prayed: "My heart rejoices in the LORD! The LORD has made me strong. Now I have an answer for my enemies; I rejoice because you rescued me. No one is holy like the LORD! There is no one besides you; there is no Rock like our God" (1 SAMUEL 2:1–2 NLT).

*Praise and prayer go hand in hand in the Bible. Hannah thanks God for answering her prayer for a child. She would dedicate her beloved son Samuel to God and he would love God as his mother did, answering God's call with, "Speak, Lord, your servant is listening" (see 1 Samuel 3:9–11).*

———

Obey the LORD your God. Follow him by obeying his demands, his commands, his laws, and his rules that are written in the teachings of Moses. If you do these things, you will be successful in all you do and wherever you go. (1 KINGS 2:3 NCV)

*Here David is nearing the end of his life. Knowing how hard it is to govern, he urges his son Solomon, who will rule after him, to obey God, which would make him successful.*

———

So David blessed the LORD in the sight of all the assembly; and David said, "Blessed are You, O LORD God of Israel our father, forever and ever. Yours, O LORD, is the greatness and the power and the glory and the victory and the majesty, indeed everything that is in the heavens and the earth; Yours is the dominion, O LORD, and You exalt Yourself as head over all. Both riches and honor come from You, and You rule over all, and in Your hand is power and might; and it lies in Your hand to make great and to strengthen everyone. Now therefore, our God, we thank You, and praise Your glorious name.

But who am I and who are my people that we should be able to offer as generously as this? For all things come from You, and from Your hand we have given You. For we are sojourners before You, and tenants, as all our fathers were; our days on the earth are like a shadow, and there is no hope. O LORD our God, all this abundance that we have provided to build You a house for Your holy name, it is from Your hand, and all is Yours. Since I know, O my God, that You try the heart and delight in uprightness, I, in the integrity of my heart, have willingly offered all these things; so now with joy I have seen Your people, who are present here, make their offerings willingly to You. O LORD, the God of Abraham, Isaac and Israel, our fathers, preserve this forever in the intentions of the heart of Your people, and direct their heart to You; and give to my son Solomon a perfect heart to keep Your commandments, Your testimonies and Your statutes, and to do them all, and to build the temple, for which I have made provision" (1 CHRONICLES 29:10–19 NASB).

> *David often combines thanksgiving with praise, a natural connection when one reflects on the goodness of God. The closer he gets to the end of his life, the more he praises God.*
>
> *The Lord's Prayer ends with similar language to that which David uses in the opening of this passage: "Yours is the kingdom and the power and the glory forever. Amen."*

———

Now, O my God, I beseech You, let Your eyes be open and Your ears attentive to the prayer offered in this temple.

So now arise, O Lord God, and come into Your resting place, You and the ark of Your strength and power. Let Your priests, O Lord God, be clothed with salvation, and let Your saints (Your zealous ones) rejoice in good and in Your goodness.

O Lord God, turn not away the face of [me] Your anointed one; [earnestly] remember Your good deeds, mercy, and steadfast love for David Your servant. (**2 CHRONICLES 6:40–42 AMP**)

> *This is Solomon's prayer of dedication of the temple. He asks for spiritual blessings, including repentance, joy, and thankfulness for all God has done. (The prayer in its entirety begins with 6:14.)*

———

O LORD, our Lord, how excellent is thy name in all the earth! who hast set thy glory above the heavens. Out of the mouth of babes and sucklings hast thou ordained strength because of thine enemies, that thou mightest still the enemy and the avenger.

When I consider thy heavens, the work of thy fingers, the moon and the stars, which thou hast ordained; what is man, that thou art mindful of him? and the son of man, that thou visitest him? For thou hast made him a little lower than the angels, and hast crowned him with glory and honour. Thou madest him to have dominion over the works of thy hands; thou hast put all things under his feet: All sheep and oxen, yea, and the beasts of the field; the fowl of the air, and the fish of the sea, and whatsoever passeth through the paths of the seas.

O LORD our Lord, how excellent is thy name in all the earth! (PSALM 8 KJV)

*This psalm is a reflection on the glory and greatness of God. It begins and ends with the same statement of the excellency of God's name. The verses in between prove that statement by examples of God's goodness to man, including making himself known to us and giving us dominion over the creatures on earth. In the hardest times of life, remembering God's goodness is critical.*

———

Praise the Lord, because he heard my prayer for help. The LORD is my strength and shield. I trust him, and he helps me. I am very happy, and I praise him with my song. The LORD is powerful; he gives victory to his chosen one.

Save your people and bless those who are your own. Be their shepherd and carry them forever. (PSALM 28:6–9 NCV)

———

How great is your goodness that you have stored up for those who fear you, that you have given to those who trust you. You do this for all to see.

You protect them by your presence from what people plan against them. You shelter them from evil words.

Praise the LORD. His love to me was wonderful when my city was attacked.

In my distress, I said, "God cannot see me!" But you heard my prayer when I cried out to you for help.

Love the LORD, all you who belong to him. The LORD protects those who truly believe, but he punishes the proud as much as they have sinned.

All you who put your hope in the LORD be strong and brave. (**PSALM 31:19–24 NCV**)

> *Despite the psalmist's dire circumstances, he appeals to God with confidence that He will help him.*

———

Many pains come to the wicked, but the one who trusts in the LORD will have faithful love surrounding him. Be glad in the LORD and rejoice, you righteous ones; shout for joy, all you upright in heart. (**PSALM 32:10–11 HCSB**)

———

For the word of the LORD is upright, and all his work is done in faithfulness. He loves righteousness and justice; the earth is full of the steadfast love of the LORD.

By the word of the LORD the heavens were made, and by the breath of his mouth all their host. He gathers the waters of the sea as a heap; he puts the deeps in storehouses.

Let all the earth fear the LORD; let all the inhabitants of the world stand in awe of him! For he spoke, and it came to be; he commanded, and it stood firm.

The LORD brings the counsel of the nations to nothing; he frustrates the plans of the peoples. The counsel of the LORD stands forever, the plans of his heart to all generations. (PSALM 33:4–11 ESV)

*Praise is the subject of this psalm. Believers are urged to praise Him for many reasons, including His character, His creation, His sovereignty, and His steadfast love. Knowing these facts about God can calm us in a time of storm, knowing He is with us and faithful to help.*

———

Do not fret because of evildoers, nor be envious of the workers of iniquity. For they shall soon be cut down like the grass, and wither as the green herb.

Trust in the LORD, and do good; dwell in the land, and feed on His faithfulness. Delight yourself also in the LORD, and He shall give you the desires of your heart.

Commit your way to the LORD, trust also in Him, and He shall bring it to pass. He shall bring forth your righteousness as the light, and your justice as the noonday.

Rest in the LORD, and wait patiently for Him; do not fret because of him who prospers in his way, because of the man who brings wicked schemes to pass. Cease from anger, and forsake wrath; do not fret—it only causes harm.

For evildoers shall be cut off; but those who wait on the LORD, they shall inherit the earth. For yet a little while and the wicked shall be no more; indeed, you will look carefully for his place, but it shall be no more.

But the meek shall inherit the earth, and shall delight themselves in the abundance of peace. The wicked plots against the just, and gnashes at him with his teeth.

The Lord laughs at him, for He sees that his day is coming. The wicked have drawn the sword and have bent their bow, to cast down the poor and needy, to slay those who are of upright conduct.

Their sword shall enter their own heart, and their bows shall be broken.

A little that a righteous man has is better than the riches of many wicked. For the arms of the wicked shall be broken, but the LORD upholds the righteous.

The LORD knows the days of the upright, and their inheritance shall be forever. They shall not be ashamed in the evil time, and in the days of famine they shall be satisfied.

But the wicked shall perish; and the enemies of the LORD, like the splendor of the meadows, shall vanish. Into smoke they shall vanish away.

The wicked borrows and does not repay, but the righteous shows mercy and gives. For those blessed by Him shall inherit the earth, but those cursed by Him shall be cut off. The steps of a good man are ordered by the LORD, and He delights in his way. Though he fall, he shall not be utterly cast down; for the LORD upholds him with His hand.

I have been young, and now am old; yet I have not seen the righteous forsaken, nor his descendants begging bread. He is ever merciful, and lends; and his descendants are blessed.

Depart from evil, and do good; and dwell forevermore. For the LORD loves justice, and does not forsake His saints; they are preserved forever, but the descendants of the wicked shall be cut off. The righteous shall inherit the land, and dwell in it forever.

The mouth of the righteous speaks wisdom, and his tongue talks of justice. The law of his God is in his heart; none of his steps shall slide.

The wicked watches the righteous, and seeks to slay him. The LORD will not leave him in his hand, nor condemn him when he is judged.

Wait on the LORD, and keep His way, and He shall exalt you to inherit the land;

When the wicked are cut off, you shall see it. I have seen the wicked in great power, and spreading himself like a native green tree. Yet he passed away, and behold, he was no more; indeed I sought him, but he could not be found.

Mark the blameless man, and observe the upright; for the future of that man is peace. But the transgressors shall be destroyed together; the future of the wicked shall be cut off.

But the salvation of the righteous is from the LORD; He is their strength in the time of trouble. And the LORD shall help them and deliver them; He shall deliver them from the wicked, and save them, because they trust in Him. (**PSALM 37** NKJV)

> *Most of us have wondered, at some time or other, why it is that evil people often seem to be so successful in terms of careers, wealth, lovely family, or good health. And we have known good-hearted individuals who have known a string of suffering. The psalmist urges us to stop thinking about this mystery and rely on the fact that eventually God will make every wrong right.*

―――――

Blessed is the one you discipline, LORD, the one you teach from your law; you grant them relief from days of trouble, till a pit is dug for the wicked. For the LORD will not reject his people; he will never forsake his inheritance. Judgment will again be founded on righteousness, and all the upright in heart will follow it.

Who will rise up for me against the wicked? Who will take a stand for me against evildoers? Unless the LORD had given me help, I would soon have dwelt in the silence of death. When I said, "My foot is slipping," your unfailing love, LORD, supported me. When anxiety was great within me, your consolation brought me joy. (**PSALM 94:12–19** NIV)

> *God uses difficulties to help us grow in grace, in faith, and in obedience, and to make us more like Jesus. Think of the wicked one who receives no correction but is allowed to wallow in his sin until it destroys him. As a loving parent disciplines a child so that the child will have a better life, our loving heavenly Parent corrects us as well.*

---

Trust in the LORD with all your heart, and do not lean on your own understanding. In all your ways acknowledge him, and he will make straight your paths.

The LORD by wisdom founded the earth; by understanding he established the heavens; by his knowledge the deeps broke open, and the clouds drop down the dew.

My son, do not lose sight of these—keep sound wisdom and discretion, and they will be life for your soul and adornment for your neck. Then you will walk on your way securely, and your foot will not stumble. If you lie down, you will not be afraid; when you lie down, your sleep will be sweet.

Do not be afraid of sudden terror or of the ruin of the wicked, when it comes, for the LORD will be your confidence and will keep your foot from being caught. (**PROVERBS 3:5-6, 19–26** ESV)

---

Are there any among the false gods of the nations that can bring rain? Or can the heavens give showers? Are you not he, O LORD our God?

We set our hope on you, for you do all these things. (**JEREMIAH 14:22** ESV)

> *How comforting to know that, even when we can't see it in the events of our lives, God is in complete control and has a plan for good and not for evil (Jeremiah 29:11).*

---

"I say this because I know what I am planning for you," says the LORD. "I have good plans for you, not plans to hurt you. I will give you hope and a good future. Then you will call my name. You will come to me and pray to me, and I will listen to you. You will search for me. And when you search for me with all your heart, you will find me!" (JEREMIAH 29:11–13 NCV)

*What a promise—hope and a good future! The key to finding God is searching and yearning for Him with all our hearts, not with lukewarm, timid, barely-interested faith. He is there; He is waiting; and He is faithful to always reveal himself when we eagerly search for Him.*

Then Jesus said to His disciples, If anyone desires to be My disciple, let him deny himself [disregard, lose sight of, and forget himself and his own interests] and take up his cross and follow Me [cleave steadfastly to Me, conform wholly to My example in living and, if need be, in dying, also].

For whoever is bent on saving his [temporal] life [his comfort and security here] shall lose it [eternal life]; and whoever loses his life [his comfort and security here] for My sake shall find it [life everlasting].

For what will it profit a man if he gains the whole world and forfeits his life [his blessed life in the kingdom of God]? Or what would a man give as an exchange for his [blessed] life [in the kingdom of God]?

For the Son of Man is going to come in the glory (majesty, splendor) of His Father with His angels, and then He will render account and reward every man in accordance with what he has done.

Truly I tell you, there are some standing here who will not taste death before they see the Son of Man coming in (into) His kingdom. (**MATTHEW 16:24–28 AMP**)

*Of course, none of us will ever take up the horrible cross that Jesus carried and then hung on when He gave His life for us. But taking up one's cross means patiently bearing the challenges, difficulties, and even disasters we experience in this life. We can imitate Jesus by bearing these things with acceptance and trust in the Lord, as He did, knowing that God has something wonderful in store for us eventually.*

———

At that time the disciples came to Jesus, saying, "Who is the greatest in the kingdom of heaven?"

And calling to him a child, he put him in the midst of them and said, "Truly, I say to you, unless you turn and become like children, you will never enter the kingdom of heaven. Whoever humbles himself like this child is the greatest in the kingdom of heaven" (**MATTHEW 18:1–4 ESV**).

*Jesus knew that the disciples were bickering among themselves as to which of them was most important. As He did so often, He turned traditional knowledge and understanding upside down by saying that the little child would be the greatest. He wants us all—regardless of age, position, education, or accomplishment—to approach Him as the children did—with open arms and delightful expectation.*

I tell you the truth, you can say to this mountain, "Go, fall into the sea." And if you have no doubts in your mind and believe that what you say will happen, God will do it for you.

So I tell you to believe that you have received the things you ask for in prayer, and God will give them to you.

When you are praying, if you are angry with someone, forgive him so that your Father in heaven will also forgive your sins.

But if you don't forgive other people, then your Father in heaven will not forgive your sins. (**MARK 11:23–26 NCV**)

> *"This mountain" refers to the Mount of Olives near where they were. And "the sea" is the Sea of Galilee. What Jesus alludes to, though, is anything as difficult as casting a mountain into the sea. We can go to God with even the most seemingly impossible things—the things that have been that way for years or even decades—knowing that they are not too hard for Him to take care of.*

I can guarantee this truth: Those who believe in me will do the things that I am doing. They will do even greater things because I am going to the Father.

I will do anything you ask the Father in my name so that the Father will be given glory because of the Son.

If you ask me to do something, I will do it.

If you love me, you will obey my commandments. (**JOHN 14:12–15 GW**)

*The greater things Jesus says the disciples will do may refer to the larger number of converts that will be made and the greater scope of carrying the gospel into the whole world, including the Gentiles. Praying in Jesus' name means praying in agreement with His purposes and will.*

———

And we know that all things work together for good to those who love God, to those who are the called according to His purpose. For whom He foreknew, He also predestined to be conformed to the image of His Son, that He might be the firstborn among many brethren. Moreover whom He predestined, these He also called; whom He called, these He also justified; and whom He justified, these He also glorified.

What then shall we say to these things? If God is for us, who can be against us? He who did not spare His own Son, but delivered Him up for us all, how shall He not with Him also freely give us all things? (**ROMANS 8:28–32 NKJV**)

*This well-known passage refers to our spiritual good—making us more like Jesus. Everything that draws us to God, breaks us free from sin, and readies us for heaven is good.*

———

Oh, the depth of the riches both of the wisdom and knowledge of God! How unsearchable are His judgments and unfathomable His ways! For WHO HAS KNOWN THE MIND OF THE LORD, OR WHO BECAME HIS COUNSELOR? (**ROMANS 11:33–34 NASB**)

———

Now the Lord is the Spirit, and where the Spirit of the Lord is, there is liberty (emancipation from bondage, freedom).

And all of us, as with unveiled face, [because we] continued to behold [in the Word of God] as in a mirror the glory of the Lord, are constantly being transfigured into His very own image in ever increasing splendor and from one degree of glory to another; [for this comes] from the Lord [Who is] the Spirit. (2 CORINTHIANS 3:17–18 AMP)

> *As we look to Jesus and contemplate His glory, we are changed because looking to Jesus has a transforming power. If we gaze at Him, we will become like Him. Remember how Moses' face shone after he had been in the Lord's presence? We also will reflect His glory as we know, love, and obey Him.*

———

To me, though I am the very least of all the saints, this grace was given, to preach to the Gentiles the unsearchable riches of Christ, and to bring to light for everyone what is the plan of the mystery hidden for ages in God who created all things, so that through the church the manifold wisdom of God might now be made known to the rulers and authorities in the heavenly places. This was according to the eternal purpose that he has realized in Christ Jesus our Lord, in whom we have boldness and access with confidence through our faith in him. So I ask you not to lose heart over what I am suffering for you, which is your glory.

For this reason I bow my knees before the Father, from whom every family in heaven and on earth is named, that according to the riches of his glory he may grant you to be strengthened with power through his Spirit in your inner being, so that Christ may dwell in your hearts through faith—that you, being rooted and grounded in love, may have strength to comprehend with all the saints what is the breadth and length and height and depth, and to know the love of Christ that surpasses knowledge, that you may be filled with all the fullness of God.

Now to him who is able to do far more abundantly than all that we ask or think, according to the power at work within us, to him be glory in the church and in Christ Jesus throughout all generations, forever and ever. Amen. (**EPHESIANS 3:8–21 ESV**)

*Paul was always humbled by remembering that he had been a persecutor of believers before he met Jesus on the road to Damascus. He is ever aware of God's grace in saving him and using him. Though Paul's sufferings were severe, he gloried in the privilege of serving Christ. His prayer for the believers here ends with the beautiful statement of praise about how God can do far more than we could ever ask or think.*

---

I am coming soon. Continue strong in your faith so no one will take away your crown. I will make those who win the victory pillars in the temple of my God, and they will never have to leave it. I will write on them the name of my God and the name of the city of my God, the new Jerusalem, that comes down out of heaven from my God. I will also write on them my new name. (**REVELATION 3:11–12 NCV**)

*The written name of God indicates character and ownership (see John 1:12). God will own these people and mold their character to become like His.*

# 7

# God's Word in Times of
# Fear

It is an issue of where we look. We can look downward in
despair and outward in fear and confusion as we survey
our circumstances. Or we can look upward to Him and
inward to our choices.[7]

—*The Upside of Down*

The Old Testament prophets looked ahead and saw God's
plan to redeem mankind through Jesus. Often the circumstances of the prophets were dire—they faced persecution,
mockery, even death. They still proclaimed their messages,
sometimes boldly, sometimes reluctantly, other times fearfully. But they shared the hope they found in God and the
future events they knew would happen. They didn't let their
fear stop them. It has been said that courage isn't the absence
of fear but acting in the midst of fear.

It can be hard to think of good things in the future when we are faced with loss or suffering. It seems to be enough to think just of today and how we will get through it. Nevertheless, great joy is coming for believers.

Peeling our eyes from our fear and lifting them upward to God is the way to find the courage to take that next step.

---

## —THE SONG OF MOSES—

Then Moses and the Israelites sang this song to the LORD:

"I will sing to the LORD. He has won a glorious victory. He has thrown horses and their riders into the sea.

The LORD is my strength and my song. He is my Savior. This is my God, and I will praise him, my father's God, and I will honor him.

The LORD is a warrior! The LORD is his name.

He has thrown Pharaoh's chariots and army into the sea. Pharaoh's best officers were drowned in the Red Sea.

The deep water covered them. They sank to the bottom like a rock.

Your right hand, O LORD, wins glory because it is strong. Your right hand, O LORD, smashes your enemies.

With your unlimited majesty, you destroyed those who attacked you. You sent out your burning anger. It burned them up like straw.

With a blast from your nostrils, the water piled up. The waves stood up like a dam. The deep water thickened in the middle of the sea.

The enemy said, 'I'll pursue them! I'll catch up with them! I'll divide the loot! I'll take all I want! I'll use my sword! I'll take all they have!'

Your breath blew the sea over them. They sank like lead in the raging water.

Who is like you among the gods, O LORD? Who is like you? You are glorious because of your holiness and awe-inspiring because of your splendor. You perform miracles. You stretched out your right hand. The earth swallowed them.

Lovingly, you will lead the people you have saved. Powerfully, you will guide them to your holy dwelling. People will hear of it and tremble. The people of Philistia will be in anguish.

The tribal leaders of Edom will be terrified. The powerful men of Moab will tremble. The people of Canaan will be deathly afraid.

Terror and dread will fall on them. Because of the power of your arm, they will be petrified until your people pass by, O LORD, until the people you purchased pass by.

You will bring them and plant them on your own mountain, the place where you live, O LORD, the holy place that you built with your own hands, O Lord.

The LORD will rule as king forever and ever."

When Pharaoh's horses, chariots, and cavalry went into the sea, the LORD made the water of the sea flow back over them. However, the Israelites had gone through the sea on dry ground. (**EXODUS 15:1–19 GW**)

*Here God is described as the king and champion who will lead
the Israelites to victory. They experience sorrow, but they have
comfort because He is their song and will be their salvation.*

―――――

The LORD will deliver them up before you, and you shall do
to them according to all the commandments which I have
commanded you. Be strong and courageous, do not be afraid
or tremble at them, for the LORD your God is the one who
goes with you. He will not fail you or forsake you.

Then Moses called to Joshua and said to him in the sight
of all Israel, "Be strong and courageous, for you shall go with
this people into the land which the LORD has sworn to their
fathers to give them, and you shall give it to them as an inheritance. The LORD is the one who goes ahead of you; He
will be with you. He will not fail you or forsake you. Do not
fear or be dismayed" (**DEUTERONOMY 31:5–8 NASB**).

*God had promised to give the Israelites victory over the Canaan-
ites, but they were to destroy all the altars and places of worship,
make no covenants with them, and not intermarry. They were to
trust in God alone for their victory, taking strength and courage
from this knowledge. The apostle seems to refer to this passage
in 1 Corinthians 16:13.*

―――――

Be strong and very courageous. Be careful to obey all the law
my servant Moses gave you; do not turn from it to the right
or to the left, that you may be successful wherever you go.
Keep this Book of the Law always on your lips; meditate on

it day and night, so that you may be careful to do everything written in it. Then you will be prosperous and successful. Have I not commanded you? Be strong and courageous. Do not be afraid; do not be discouraged, for the LORD your God will be with you wherever you go. (JOSHUA 1:7–9 NIV)

*Again, we have a call for courage and obedience as essential to victory. Canaan would belong to the Israelites since God was giving it to them. Here we see that, despite this assurance, Joshua's courage and hope of victory still depended on his obedience.*

———

Blessed be the LORD who has given rest to his people Israel, according to all that he promised. Not one word has failed of all his good promise, which he spoke by Moses his servant. The LORD our God be with us, as he was with our fathers. May he not leave us or forsake us, that he may incline our hearts to him, to walk in all his ways and to keep his commandments, his statutes, and his rules, which he commanded our fathers. Let these words of mine, with which I have pleaded before the LORD, be near to the LORD our God day and night, and may he maintain the cause of his servant and the cause of his people Israel, as each day requires, that all the peoples of the earth may know that the LORD is God; there is no other. Let your heart therefore be wholly true to the LORD our God, walking in his statutes and keeping his commandments, as at this day. (1 KINGS 8:56–61 ESV)

*Solomon knows that humans cannot achieve sinless perfection, but as he praises God, he asks that the people would be wholeheartedly for God, single-minded, and sincere in their love for Him.*

————

O LORD, God of our fathers, are you not God in heaven? You rule over all the kingdoms of the nations. In your hand are power and might, so that none is able to withstand you. (**2 CHRONICLES 20:6** ESV)

*God's sovereignty is infinite, unlimited, and uncontrollable. No man, no army, no nation can thwart His purposes. Here Jehoshaphat, king of Judah, sought God as his enemies attacked.*

————

But You, LORD, are a shield around me, my glory, and the One who lifts up my head. I cry aloud to the LORD, and He answers me from His holy mountain. I lie down and sleep; I wake again because the LORD sustains me. I am not afraid of the thousands of people who have taken their stand against me on every side. (**PSALM 3:3–6** HCSB)

*David is considered to be the writer of about half of the psalms in the book of Psalms. Here, although he is in great distress, at the same time he begs God for help, he anticipates that He will surely come to his aid. His certainty leads to confidence and praise.*

————

Do not be so far away, O LORD. Come quickly to help me, O my strength. Rescue my soul from the sword, my life from vicious dogs. Save me from the mouth of the lion and from the horns of wild oxen.

You have answered me. I will tell my people about your name. I will praise you within the congregation. All who fear the LORD, praise him! All you descendants of Jacob, glorify him! Stand in awe of him, all you descendants of Israel.

The LORD has not despised or been disgusted with the plight of the oppressed one. He has not hidden his face from that person. The LORD heard when that oppressed person cried out to him for help.

My praise comes from you while I am among those assembled for worship. I will fulfill my vows in the presence of those who fear the LORD. Oppressed people will eat until they are full. Those who look to the LORD will praise him. May you live forever.

All the ends of the earth will remember and return to the LORD. All the families from all the nations will worship you because the kingdom belongs to the LORD and he rules the nations.

All prosperous people on earth will eat and worship. All those who go down to the dust will kneel in front of him, even those who are barely alive. There will be descendants who serve him, a generation that will be told about the Lord. They will tell people yet to be born about his righteousness—that he has finished it. (PSALM 22:19–31 GW)

*No matter what the circumstance, we can call out to God and He will help us. From one generation to another, believers must remember and recount His goodness and the many times He saves and helps us. Like the psalmist, we too may feel overwhelmed, terrified, and grief-stricken. But as we remember times of God's faithfulness in the past, we can summon the courage to face yet another trial.*

———

The LORD *is* my light and my salvation; whom shall I fear? The LORD is the strength of my life; of whom shall I be afraid?

One thing I have desired of the LORD, that will I seek: that I may dwell in the house of the LORD all the days of my life, to behold the beauty of the LORD, and to inquire in His temple. For in the time of trouble He shall hide me in His pavilion; in the secret place of His tabernacle He shall hide me; He shall set me high upon a rock.

And now my head shall be lifted up above my enemies all around me; therefore I will offer sacrifices of joy in His tabernacle; I will sing, yes, I will sing praises to the LORD.

Hear, O LORD, when I cry with my voice! Have mercy also upon me, and answer me. When You said, "Seek My face," My heart said to You, "Your face, LORD, I will seek." Do not hide Your face from me; do not turn Your servant away in anger; You have been my help; do not leave me nor forsake me, O God of my salvation. When my father and my mother forsake me, then the LORD will take care of me.

Teach me Your way, O LORD, and lead me in a smooth path, because of my enemies. Do not deliver me to the will of my adversaries; for false witnesses have risen against me, and such as breathe out violence. I would have lost heart, unless I had believed that I would see the goodness of the LORD in the land of the living.

Wait on the LORD; be of good courage, and He shall strengthen your heart; wait, I say, on the LORD! **(PSALM 27:1, 4–14 NKJV)**

*Some think this psalm was written when David was fleeing from Saul, who had turned against him because of jealousy and an evil spirit's influence. Although David is surrounded by enemies, he chooses to wait on the Lord for strength.*

———

God is our protection and our strength. He always helps in times of trouble. So we will not be afraid even if the earth shakes, or the mountains fall into the sea, even if the oceans roar and foam, or the mountains shake at the raging sea. **(PSALM 46:1–3 NCV)**

———

Praise the LORD! Blessed is the man who fears the LORD, who greatly delights in his commandments! His offspring will be mighty in the land; the generation of the upright will be blessed. Wealth and riches are in his house, and his righteousness endures forever.

Light dawns in the darkness for the upright; he is gracious, merciful, and righteous.

It is well with the man who deals generously and lends; who conducts his affairs with justice. For the righteous will never be moved; he will be remembered forever.

He is not afraid of bad news; his heart is firm, trusting in the LORD. His heart is steady; he will not be afraid, until he looks in triumph on his adversaries.

He has distributed freely; he has given to the poor; his righteousness endures forever; his horn is exalted in honor. **(PSALM 112:1–9 ESV)**

*Knowing that God is unchangeable and that He loves us and wants the best for us, we don't have to fear anyone or anything. The man described here is not afraid of bad news and such a state demonstrates an amazing confidence. Such confidence is only possible when we are anchored on a Rock that cannot be moved.*

———

The name of the LORD is a fortified tower; the righteous run to it and are safe. **(PROVERBS 18:10 NIV)**

———

Fear of the LORD leads to life, bringing security and protection from harm. **(PROVERBS 19:23 NLT)**

———

Every word of God is flawless; he is a shield to those who take refuge in him. **(PROVERBS 30:5 NIV)**

———

Surely God is my salvation; I will trust and not be afraid. The LORD, the LORD himself, is my strength and my defense; he has become my salvation.

With joy you will draw water from the wells of salvation.

In that day you will say: "Give praise to the LORD, proclaim his name; make known among the nations what he has done, and proclaim that his name is exalted.

"Sing to the LORD, for he has done glorious things; let this be known to all the world. Shout aloud and sing for joy, people of Zion, for great is the Holy One of Israel among you" (ISAIAH 12:2–6 NIV).

*This hymn of praise offers a promise that we will find peace and joy when we believe in God and when we turn from sin in repentance. Our faith can overcome our fear when we remember and rely on God's promises and His faithfulness in the past.*

―――――

With perfect peace you will protect those whose minds cannot be changed, because they trust you.

Trust the LORD always, because the LORD, the LORD alone, is an everlasting rock. (ISAIAH 26:3–4 GW)

―――――

So don't worry, because I am with you. Don't be afraid, because I am your God. I will make you strong and will help you; I will support you with my right hand that saves you.

All those people who are angry with you will be ashamed and disgraced. Those who are against you will disappear and be lost. You will look for your enemies, but you will not find them. Those who fought against you will vanish completely.

I am the LORD your God, who holds your right hand, and I tell you, "Don't be afraid. I will help you. You few people of Israel who are left, do not be afraid even though you are weak as a worm. I myself will help you," says the LORD. "The one who saves you is the Holy One of Israel. Look, I have made you like a new threshing board with many sharp teeth. So you will walk on mountains and crush them; you will make the hills like chaff. You will throw them into the air, and the wind will carry them away; a windstorm will scatter them.

"Then you will be happy in the LORD; you will be proud of the Holy One of Israel. The poor and needy people look for water, but they can't find any. Their tongues are dry with thirst. But I, the Lord, will answer their prayers; I, the God of Israel, will not leave them to die. I will make rivers flow on the dry hills and springs flow through the valleys. I will change the desert into a lake of water and the dry land into fountains of water. I will make trees grow in the desert—cedars, acacia, myrtle, and olive trees. I will put pine, fir, and cypress trees growing together in the desert" (ISAIAH 41:10–19 NCV).

*These promises are fulfilled in Christ, who gives all believers victory over the powers of darkness. God will answer our prayers, sometimes not in the way we would wish, but He can see the end from the beginning, which we cannot, and knows what is best. Joshua 1:9 is another encouragement for us to rely on God and not to fear. "Remember that I commanded you to be strong and brave. Don't be afraid, because the LORD your God will be with you everywhere you go."*

---

Do not fear, for I have redeemed you; I have called you by name; you are Mine! When you pass through the waters, I will be with you; and through the rivers, they will not overflow you. When you walk through the fire, you will not be scorched, nor will the flame burn you. For I am the Lord your God, the Holy One of Israel, your Savior. (ISAIAH 43:1–3 NASB)

*Again we are exhorted to fear not. By water and fire the prophet means all kinds of trouble and danger. But we are His! God delights in His people. If He is for us, whom should we fear? Who is stronger, more powerful than He?*

————

Now on the last day, the great day of the feast, Jesus stood and cried out, saying, "If anyone is thirsty, let him come to Me and drink.

He who believes in Me, as the Scripture said, 'From his innermost being shall flow rivers of living water' " (**JOHN 7:37–38 NASB**).

*One of the many Old Testament prophecies about Jesus is in Jeremiah 17:13: "O LORD, the hope of Israel; all who forsake you will be put to shame. Those who turn away from you will be written in the dust because they have forsaken the LORD, the spring of living water." (See also Isaiah 58:11.)*

————

So Jesus said to them again, "Truly, truly, I say to you, I am the door of the sheep. All who came before Me are thieves and robbers, but the sheep did not hear them. I am the door; if anyone enters through Me, he will be saved, and will go in and out and find pasture. The thief comes only to steal and kill and destroy; I came that they may have life, and have it abundantly.

"I am the good shepherd; the good shepherd lays down His life for the sheep. He who is a hired hand, and not a shepherd, who is not the owner of the sheep, sees the wolf coming, and leaves the sheep and flees, and the wolf snatches them and scatters them. He flees because he is a hired hand and is not concerned about the sheep. I am the good shepherd, and I know My own and My own know Me, even as the Father knows Me and I know the Father; and I lay down My life for the sheep. I have other sheep, which are not of this fold; I must bring them also, and they will hear My voice; and they will become one flock with one shepherd. For this reason the Father loves Me, because I lay down My life so that I may take it again. No one has taken it away from Me, but I lay it down on My own initiative. I have authority to lay it down, and I have authority to take it up again. This commandment I received from My Father" (JOHN 10:7–18 NASB).

*As the door for the sheep, Jesus ushers them into protection and safety. The thieves and robbers refer to those who either pretend to be the Messiah or in another way lead people away from God. Here He also refers to the Jewish religious leaders who cared only about their rules and reputations and not about the spiritual lives of the people.*

Jesus answered and said to him, "If anyone loves Me, he will keep My word; and My Father will love him, and We will come to him and make Our home with him.

He who does not love Me does not keep My words; and the word which you hear is not Mine but the Father's who sent Me.

These things I have spoken to you while being present with you. But the Helper, the Holy Spirit, whom the Father will send in My name, He will teach you all things, and bring to your remembrance all things that I said to you.

Peace I leave with you, My peace I give to you; not as the world gives do I give to you. Let not your heart be troubled, neither let it be afraid.

You have heard Me say to you, 'I am going away and coming back to you.' If you loved Me, you would rejoice because I said, 'I am going to the Father,' for My Father is greater than I" (JOHN 14:23–28 NKJV).

> *The peace Jesus promised to His disciples was the peace Jesus himself possessed while on earth, peace from within regardless of His circumstances or enemies. It is an inner calm in the midst of the storm.*

———

Dear friends, we must love each other because love comes from God. Everyone who loves has been born from God and knows God. The person who doesn't love doesn't know God, because God is love.

God has shown us his love by sending his only Son into the world so that we could have life through him. This is love: not that we have loved God, but that he loved us and sent his Son to be the payment for our sins.

Dear friends, if this is the way God loved us, we must also love each other. No one has ever seen God. If we love each other, God lives in us, and his love is perfected in us. We know that we live in him and he lives in us because he has given us his Spirit.

We have seen and testify to the fact that the Father sent his Son as the Savior of the world. God lives in those who declare that Jesus is the Son of God, and they live in God. We have known and believed that God loves us. God is love. Those who live in God's love live in God, and God lives in them.

God's love has reached its goal in us. So we look ahead with confidence to the day of judgment. While we are in this world, we are exactly like him with regard to love. No fear exists where his love is. Rather, perfect love gets rid of fear, because fear involves punishment. The person who lives in fear doesn't have perfect love.

We love because God loved us first. (1 JOHN 4:7–19 GW)

*Love shows others that we know and love God. If we are of God, and God loves us, we must love one another. And love has another astounding benefit—it chases away fear!*

———

Then the seventh angel blew his trumpet, and there were loud voices in heaven, saying, "The kingdom of the world has become the kingdom of our Lord and of his Christ, and he shall reign forever and ever."

And the twenty-four elders who sit on their thrones before God fell on their faces and worshiped God, saying,

"We give thanks to you, Lord God Almighty, who is and who was, for you have taken your great power and begun to reign. The nations raged, but your wrath came, and the time for the dead to be judged, and for rewarding your servants, the prophets and saints, and those who fear your name, both small and great, and for destroying the destroyers of the earth."

Then God's temple in heaven was opened, and the ark of his covenant was seen within his temple. There were flashes of lightning, rumblings, peals of thunder, an earthquake, and heavy hail. (**REVELATION 11:15–19 ESV**)

> *Can't you just hear the glorious music of Handel's Messiah when you read these words in Revelation? The seventh trumpet proclaims the victory and permanent reign of Christ. This brings one series of visions—from John's time to the end of the world—to a close.*

# 8

## God's Word in Times of
# Need

I began to wonder if God's promises had any real meaning. Finally one day I said to God, "I will take You at Your Word. I will believe that in Your time and in Your way, You will deliver me." The difficulties did not cease, but the peace of God did quiet my fears and anxieties. And then, in due time, God did deliver me from those troubles, and He did it in such a way that I knew He had done it. God's promises are true. They cannot fail because He cannot lie. But, to realize the peace they are intended to give, we must choose to believe them. We must cast our anxieties upon him.[8]

—*Trusting God Even When Life Hurts*

When we are dealing with unmet needs, God and His promises can seem far away. After all, didn't He promise to provide what we need? At the times when we need them most, His words of comfort and assurance can be hard to grab hold of and believe. But that's when it's most important to cling to God and His Word and to decide that we believe what He says even when we don't feel like it—even when we have a serious need and seemingly no way to meet it.

If we can believe Him and obey Him in those times when it seems impossible to do, our feelings will eventually catch up with our obedience. God keeps His promises, and we discover that truth by slowly, painstakingly stepping toward Him and away from our fear.

God was faithful, gracious, and merciful to His people in the Bible. Trust Him and see how His love and grace are also available to us today.

The LORD said to Moses, "Tell Aaron and his sons, 'This is how you should bless the Israelites. Say to them: "May the LORD bless you and keep you. May the LORD show you his kindness and have mercy on you. May the LORD watch over you and give you peace."'

"So Aaron and his sons will bless the Israelites with my name, and I will bless them" (NUMBERS 6:22–27 NCV).

*Here the priests are appointed to bless the people in the name of the Lord as part of their work. With these instructions, God honors the priests and comforts the people, who considered the priests as God's messengers to them.*

When you have eaten and are satisfied, you shall bless the LORD your God for the good land which He has given you.

Beware that you do not forget the LORD your God by not keeping His commandments and His ordinances and His statutes which I am commanding you today; otherwise, when you have eaten and are satisfied, and have built good houses and lived in them, and when your herds and your flocks multiply, and your silver and gold multiply, and all that you have multiplies, then your heart will become proud and you will forget the LORD your God who brought you out from the land of Egypt, out of the house of slavery.

He led you through the great and terrible wilderness, with its fiery serpents and scorpions and thirsty ground where there was no water; He brought water for you out of the rock of flint. In the wilderness He fed you manna which your fathers did not know, that He might humble you and that He might test you, to do good for you in the end.

Otherwise, you may say in your heart, "My power and the strength of my hand made me this wealth." But you shall remember the LORD your God, for it is He who is giving you power to make wealth, that He may confirm His covenant which He swore to your fathers, as it is this day. (**DEUTERONOMY 8:10–18 NASB**)

*Moses reminds the people of God's goodness, reciting how He provided for them in the wilderness. He warns them not to forget that it was the Lord who did all this for them so that they don't become boastful and proud and again turn from God.*

He executes justice for the fatherless and the widow, and loves the foreigner, giving him food and clothing. (**DEUTER-ONOMY 10:18 HCSB**)

*Those who have no one to help them and no resources with which to help themselves still have God as their defender and provider.*

———

And the word of the Lord came to him [Elijah]: Arise, go to Zarephath, which belongs to Sidon, and dwell there. Behold, I have commanded a widow there to provide for you.

So he arose and went to Zarephath. When he came to the gate of the city, behold, a widow was there gathering sticks. He called to her, Bring me a little water in a vessel, that I may drink.

As she was going to get it, he called to her and said, Bring me a morsel of bread in your hand.

And she said, As the Lord your God lives, I have not a loaf baked but only a handful of meal in the jar and a little oil in the bottle. See, I am gathering two sticks, that I may go in and bake it for me and my son, that we may eat it—and die.

Elijah said to her, Fear not; go and do as you have said. But make me a little cake of [it] first and bring it to me, and afterward prepare some for yourself and your son. For thus says the Lord, the God of Israel: The jar of meal shall not waste away or the bottle of oil fail until the day that the Lord sends rain on the earth.

She did as Elijah said. And she and he and her household ate for many days.

The jar of meal was not spent nor did the bottle of oil fail, according to the word which the Lord spoke through Elijah. (**1 KINGS 17:8–16 AMP**)

*Elijah's faith is greatly tested when he learns from this woman God has appointed to provide for him that her food is about to run out. She, too, doesn't know where her next meal or that of her son will come from when she uses the last of her supplies in obedience to God. She is amply rewarded when her bit of food miraculously lasts.*

---

Then Job answered the LORD and said: "I know that you can do all things, and that no purpose of yours can be thwarted. 'Who is this that hides counsel without knowledge?' Therefore I have uttered what I did not understand, things too wonderful for me, which I did not know. 'Hear, and I will speak; I will question you, and you make it known to me.'

I had heard of you by the hearing of the ear, but now my eye sees you" (**JOB 42:1–5 ESV**).

*Job uses God's own words to express his new staggering awareness of God's power, wisdom, and goodness. He is humbled as he understands his own limited human knowledge. Though he has lost everything, he is assured that God does what is best, no matter how much it might hurt at the time. He has seen spiritually what he has until now only heard about God.*

---

I know that the LORD will maintain the cause of the afflicted, and will execute justice for the needy. Surely the righteous shall give thanks to your name; the upright shall dwell in your presence. (PSALM 140:12–13 ESV)

———

The Lord is gracious and full of compassion, slow to anger and abounding in mercy and loving-kindness.

The Lord is good to all, and His tender mercies are over all His works [the entirety of things created].

All Your works shall praise You, O Lord, and Your loving ones shall bless You [affectionately and gratefully shall Your saints confess and praise You]!

They shall speak of the glory of Your kingdom and talk of Your power, To make known to the sons of men God's mighty deeds and the glorious majesty of His kingdom.

Your kingdom is an everlasting kingdom, and Your dominion endures throughout all generations.

The Lord upholds all those [of His own] who are falling and raises up all those who are bowed down.

The eyes of all wait for You [looking, watching, and expecting] and You give them their food in due season.

You open Your hand and satisfy every living thing with favor.

The Lord is [rigidly] righteous in all His ways and gracious and merciful in all His works.

The Lord is near to all who call upon Him, to all who call upon Him sincerely and in truth. He will fulfill the desires of those who reverently and worshipfully fear Him; He also will hear their cry and will save them.

The Lord preserves all those who love Him, but all the wicked will He destroy.

My mouth shall speak the praise of the Lord; and let all flesh bless (affectionately and gratefully praise) His holy name forever and ever. (**PSALM 145:8–21 AMP**)

> *This psalm shows us that those who keep praying and clinging to God in times of trouble will eventually experience the joy that displays itself in fervent praise—for God's power, goodness, mercy, and care of those who love Him.*

Better is a little with righteousness, than vast revenues without justice. (**PROVERBS 16:8 NKJV**)

Call to Me and I will answer you and tell you great and incomprehensible things you do not know. (**JEREMIAH 33:3 HCSB**)

> *God urges Jeremiah, representing the people of God, to pray and watch what God would do. Job had found that God's ways are beyond finding out because they are too wonderful for mere man to fathom. But despite the tragedies he had endured, his faith was strengthened. "I had heard of you by the hearing of the ear, but now my eye sees you." Often God's answers show us more of himself. (Refer again to Job 42:1–5.)*

And the threshing floors will be full of grain; the barrels will overflow with new wine and olive oil.

Though I sent my great army against you—those swarming locusts and hopping locusts, the destroying locusts and the cutting locusts that ate your crops—I will pay you back for those years of trouble.

Then you will have plenty to eat and be full. You will praise the name of the LORD your God, who has done miracles for you. My people will never again be shamed. Then you will know that I am among the people of Israel, that I am the LORD your God, and there is no other God. My people will never be shamed again.

After this, I will pour out my Spirit on all kinds of people. Your sons and daughters will prophesy, your old men will dream dreams, and your young men will see visions.

At that time I will pour out my Spirit also on male slaves and female slaves. I will show miracles in the sky and on the earth: blood, fire, and thick smoke.

The sun will become dark, the moon red as blood, before the overwhelming and terrible day of the LORD comes.

Then anyone who calls on the LORD will be saved, because on Mount Zion and in Jerusalem there will be people who will be saved, just as the LORD has said. Those left alive after the day of punishment are the people whom the LORD called. ( JOEL 2:24–32 NCV)

*The three ways God revealed His will in the Old Testament were through prophecy, dreams, and visions. All three are mentioned here as a full manifestation of God to His people, to be imparted by the Holy Spirit who indwells all believers in Christ. In the New*

*Testament, prophesying means speaking under the guidance of the Holy Spirit.*

———

Though the fig tree should not blossom
And there be no fruit on the vines,
Though the yield of the olive should fail
And the fields produce no food,
Though the flock should be cut off from the fold
And there be no cattle in the stalls,
Yet I will exult in the LORD,
I will rejoice in the God of my salvation.
The Lord GOD is my strength,
And He has made my feet like hinds' feet,
And makes me walk on my high places. (**HABAKKUK 3:17–19 NASB**)

*God never wastes our pain. We must hang on to one thing: God. We can say, even in the worst of times, "I may not know everything, but I know He loves me."*

———

You are the salt of the earth, but if salt has lost its taste (its strength, its quality), how can its saltness be restored? It is not good for anything any longer but to be thrown out and trodden underfoot by men.

You are the light of the world. A city set on a hill cannot be hidden.

Nor do men light a lamp and put it under a peck measure, but on a lampstand, and it gives light to all in the house.

Let your light so shine before men that they may see your moral excellence and your praiseworthy, noble, and good deeds and recognize and honor and praise and glorify your Father Who is in heaven.

Do not think that I have come to do away with or undo the Law or the Prophets; I have come not to do away with or undo but to complete and fulfill them. (**MATTHEW 5:13–17 AMP**)

*Salt is used to preserve, enhance, or bring out flavor. It can even melt ice on the roads after a snowstorm. As believers, we are to be "flavorful" and lively people who accurately portray the gospel so that others might come to know Jesus. If our flavor is gone, or if our light is hidden under a basket, we are not useful as representatives of Christ to a needy world. Even when we are hurting, we can continue to "salt" the earth with His praise.*

## —DO NOT BE ANXIOUS—

Therefore I tell you, do not be anxious about your life, what you will eat or what you will drink, nor about your body, what you will put on. Is not life more than food, and the body more than clothing?

Look at the birds of the air: they neither sow nor reap nor gather into barns, and yet your heavenly Father feeds them. Are you not of more value than they?

And which of you by being anxious can add a single hour to his span of life?

And why are you anxious about clothing? Consider the lilies of the field, how they grow: they neither toil nor spin, yet I tell you, even Solomon in all his glory was not arrayed like one of these.

But if God so clothes the grass of the field, which today is alive and tomorrow is thrown into the oven, will he not much more clothe you, O you of little faith?

Therefore do not be anxious, saying, "What shall we eat?" or "What shall we drink?" or "What shall we wear?"

For the Gentiles seek after all these things, and your heavenly Father knows that you need them all.

But seek first the kingdom of God and his righteousness, and all these things will be added to you.

Therefore do not be anxious about tomorrow, for tomorrow will be anxious for itself. Sufficient for the day is its own trouble. (MATTHEW 6:25–34 ESV)

*Jesus does not forbid working to maintain, support, and preserve our lives; nor does He tell us to give no thought or care to our work and provision. But when we despair and panic about our physical or financial needs, we show that we aren't really counting on God to provide for us. We must work hard and then let God do the rest because He knows better than we do what we really need.*

———

Ask and it will be given to you; seek and you will find; knock and the door will be opened to you.

For everyone who asks receives; the one who seeks finds; and to the one who knocks, the door will be opened.

Which of you, if your son asks for bread, will give him a stone?

Or if he asks for a fish, will give him a snake?

If you, then, though you are evil, know how to give good gifts to your children, how much more will your Father in heaven give good gifts to those who ask him! So in everything, do to others what you would have them do to you, for this sums up the Law and the Prophets. (MATTHEW 7:7–12 NIV)

*This passage underscores the importance of prayer—prayer offered in faith and thankful expectation. We know that God will answer in His way, which is always the best way even if it doesn't feel that way at the moment. Here, as elsewhere in the Bible, God promises to hear us, answer us, and take care of us.*

———

Hitherto have ye asked nothing in my name: ask, and ye shall receive, that your joy may be full.

These things have I spoken unto you in proverbs: but the time cometh, when I shall no more speak unto you in proverbs, but I shall shew you plainly of the Father.

At that day ye shall ask in my name: and I say not unto you, that I will pray the Father for you:

For the Father himself loveth you, because ye have loved me, and have believed that I came out from God.

I came forth from the Father, and am come into the world: again, I leave the world, and go to the Father. (JOHN 16:24–28 KJV)

*Jesus prepared the disciples for having direct access to the Father in prayer after His death and resurrection. Jesus still makes intercession for us (intervening on our behalf, Romans 8:34), and we can also go straight to the Father in Jesus' name.*

———

But godliness actually is a means of great gain, when accompanied by contentment. (**1 TIMOTHY 6:6** NASB)

*Sometimes we think that if and when we have everything we need or want in a material, health, or relationship sense, we will be content. But this verse says that being contented with a godly life provides the greatest gain in eternity. In Philippians 4:12, Paul said he had learned how to be content in every situation, whether in plenty or in want.*

# Notes

1. Nancy Guthrie, *Holding on to Hope* (Wheaton, IL: Tyndale House, 2002), 24.

2. Sarah Young, *Jesus Calling* (Nashville: Integrity Publishers, 2004), 222.

3. Phillip W. Keller, *A Shepherd Looks at Psalm 23* (Grand Rapids, MI: Zondervan, 1970), 86.

4. Ravi Zacharias, *Cries of the Heart* (Nashville: Word Publishing, 1998), 93.

5. Charles R. Swindoll, *Laugh Again* (Dallas: Word Publishing, 1991), 23.

6. Robert Bugh, *When the Bottom Drops Out* (Carol Stream, IL: Tyndale, 2011), 91–92.

7. Joseph M. Stowell, *The Upside of Down* (Chicago: Moody Press, 1991), 28.

8. Jerry Bridges, *Trusting God Even When Life Hurts* (Colorado Springs: NavPress, 1998), 200.